T0273863

ON
SETTLER COLONIALISM

ON

SETTLER COLONIALISM

Ideology, Violence, and Justice

ADAM KIRSCH

W. W. NORTON & COMPANY

Independent Publishers Since 1923

For information about permission to reproduce selections from this book,
write to Permissions, W. W. Norton & Company, Inc., 500 Fifth Avenue,
New York, NY 10110

For information about special discounts for bulk purchases, please contact
W. W. Norton Special Sales at specialsales@wwnorton.com or 800-233-4830

Manufacturing by Lakeside Book Company
Book design by Chris Welch
Production manager: Julia Druskin

ISBN 978-1-324-10534-3

W. W. Norton & Company, Inc., 500 Fifth Avenue, New York, NY 10110
www.wwnorton.com

W. W. Norton & Company Ltd., 15 Carlisle Street, London W1D 3BS

10 9 8 7 6 5 4 3 2 1

CONTENTS

Preface   ix

1   The Theory of a Massacre   1

2   Redefining Colonialism   15

3   A New American Countermyth   35

4   Settler Ways of Being   57

5   The Palestine Paradigm   77

6   Why Israel Can't Be Decolonized   103

7   Justice and Despair   119

Notes   133
Selected Bibliography   141

PREFACE

The crisis that began last October 7, when Hamas terrorists infiltrated Israel and killed some twelve hundred
people, is still ongoing as of this writing, six months later.
Every aspect of that crisis has been extensively analyzed in
real time: not only the atrocity in Israel and the death and
suffering caused by Israel's invasion of the Gaza Strip, but
the response of governments and institutions around the
world, the intense outrage of pro-Palestinian protesters,
and the rise in anti-Zionism and anti-Semitism. From the
start, it has been clear that these are history-making events
whose full impact will take a long time to unfold and even
longer to understand—other than to say that, like almost
all events important enough to make history, it would be
far better if they had never happened.

As a writer on Jewish literature and ideas, I've often tried to think about the role of Israel in Jewish history. But I do not write about Israeli politics or the Israeli-Palestinian conflict, and while this book responds to current events, it does not make any arguments about the conduct of the war or how the larger conflict should be resolved (though in Chapter 6, I do discuss what I think should not happen—namely, the expulsion of either Jews or Arabs).

Instead, the book focuses on one particular strand of the complex cultural-political argument surrounding Israel and Palestine: the idea of settler colonialism. While much of the general public was first introduced to this term after October 7, when it was invoked by apologists for the Hamas attack, settler colonialism has been an influential concept among academics and activists for two decades, and it is about much more than the Middle East. Originally, it is a theory about the United States, Canada, and Australia, countries that were founded by European settlers on land taken from indigenous peoples.

To put it briefly and as neutrally as possible, describing the United States and Israel as settler colonial societies is a way of arguing that they are permanently illegitimate, because they were created against the will of the people previously living there—Native Americans and Palestinian Arabs. As I will show, this principle has important consequences for the way its adherents think about the history and future of both countries, and about a number of key political issues. For this reason, I argue that settler colonialism is best understood not as a historical concept but as an ideology, whose growing popularity among educated young Americans is already having significant political effects.

My goal is to offer a critical introduction to the ideology of settler colonialism as elaborated in the work of theorists, writers, and activists. Focusing on ideas, not individuals or institutions, I look at how this way of thinking developed, what it has to say about America and Israel, and why it falls prey to some of the same crucial errors as earlier radical ideologies. Indeed, the main reason why I believe it's important to reckon with the idea of settler colonialism is that I see it leading people who think of themselves as idealists into morally disastrous territory, in ways that are all too familiar in modern history.

Finally, at the end of the book I try to suggest an alternative way of thinking about historical injustice that is both more truthful and more conducive to a better future. In a time of terrible grief and anger, the ideas discussed here may seem abstract; but in the long term, nothing does more than our ideas to determine the ways we feel and act.

April 2024

ON
SETTLER COLONIALISM

1

The Theory of a Massacre

The Hamas attack on Israel on October 7, 2023, revealed a seismic change in the way young people in the United States think about Israel and Palestine. A poll conducted two months after the attack found that while Americans as a whole supported Israel over Hamas by 81 percent to 19 percent, those aged 18–24 were split fifty-fifty.[1] Within that age group, 66 percent of respondents agreed that Hamas's attack was "genocidal in nature," yet 60 percent also said it "can be justified by the grievances of the Palestinians." In other words, more than half of college-age Americans seem to believe that it would be justified for Palestinians to commit a genocide of Israeli Jews.

The October 7 attack was perfectly calculated to crystallize this momentous shift in American opinion, because it reversed the usual terms of the Israeli-Palestinian conflict. Since Hamas, an Islamist political movement, took power in the Gaza Strip in 2007, it has fought several brief but costly battles with Israel. Until 2023, these conflicts followed the same pattern: Hamas fired rockets at Israeli towns near the Gaza border, and Israel responded with artillery shelling and airstrikes. Each time, the disproportion in firepower meant that far more Palestinians were killed than Israelis, provoking criticism of Israel around the world. During Israel's Operation Cast Lead, in December 2008, about 1,400 Palestinians were killed, and nine Israelis. During Operation Protective Edge in July and August 2014, about 2,100 Palestinians were killed, and seventy-two Israelis. And in Operation Guardian of the Walls, in May 2021, 232 Palestinians were killed, and eight Israelis.

This pattern changed dramatically on October 7, when Hamas fighters infiltrated into Israel and indiscriminately killed some 1,200 people, while taking more than 250 hostages. The attack killed four times as many Israelis in a single day as in the previous fifteen years of conflict put together. As details emerged, including bodycam footage taken by Hamas fighters, the world heard accounts of torture, mutilation, and rape, with victims including soldiers and civilians, men and women, children and the elderly.

If earlier pro-Palestinian protests had been fueled by sympathy for the victims of Israeli violence, it might be expected that after October 7, expressions of support for Hamas's violence would be muted. In fact, exactly the opposite happened: in the United States, the massacre inspired a larger and louder pro-Palestinian response than any previous conflict.

In the months that followed, some of that response took the traditional form of humanitarian protest against Israel's retaliatory invasion of Gaza, which as in previous conflicts resulted in highly disproportionate casualties. But the new tone could be heard from the moment news of the Hamas attacks arrived, well before the Israeli response began. Excitement and enthusiasm over Hamas's exploit would have been par for the course in Gaza or the West Bank, Cairo or Damascus; now it was coming from Ivy League campuses, the Democratic Socialists of America, and Black Lives Matter.

Pro-Hamas statements from students and faculty at elite schools received the most media attention. Yale professor Zareena Grewal posted on X (formerly known as Twitter), "Israel is a murderous, genocidal settler state and Palestinians have every right to resist through armed struggle, solidarity #FreePalestine."[2] The prominent Palestinian intellectual Joseph Massad, a professor at Columbia University, wrote in an article, "Perhaps the major achievement of the resistance in the temporary takeover of these settler-colonies is the death blow to any confidence that Israeli colonists had in their military and its ability to protect them."[3]

Outside the academy, many activist organizations made similar statements. The Movement for Black Lives responded to the Hamas attack by demanding "an

immediate end to Israel's lethal settler-colonial project,"
while the Salt Lake City chapter of Democratic Socialists of America issued a call "to stand up against settler-
colonial, Zionist apartheid." Progressive and anti-Zionist
publications followed suit. In *Mondoweiss*, Jeffrey Sacks
of UC Riverside justified the attack on the grounds that
"Palestinians are a non-white, non-European people
struggling for liberation and freedom against a settler
colonial oppressor."[4]

Two things about these statements are immediately
striking. The first is their frank enthusiasm for violence
against Israeli civilians. During earlier conflicts, public statements in support of Palestine typically focused
on the horror of violence and the need to protect civilian lives. During the 2014 war, for instance, *The Lancet*, a British medical journal, published an open letter in
which twenty-four doctors and scientists declared: "We
are appalled by the military onslaught on civilians in Gaza
under the guise of punishing terrorists . . . the death toll
is borne mainly by innocent people in Gaza, especially
women and children."[5]

In 2023, by contrast, the killing of Israeli civilians was
welcomed by many Palestinian sympathizers. "This is what
it means to Free Palestine," declared National Students for
Justice in Palestine: "Not just slogans and rallies, but armed
confrontation with the oppressors." These were pointedly
not the usual calls—liberal, humane, and ineffectual—for
a solution to the Israel–Palestine conflict. They were calls

for the destruction of Israel, with many activists adopting the slogan "From the River to the Sea, Palestine Will Be Free," which envisions the elimination of the Jewish state.

The second notable feature of these statements is the ubiquity of the term *settler colonial*. For many academics and activists, describing Israel as a settler colonial state was a sufficient justification for the Hamas attack, because for them the term encapsulates a whole series of ideological convictions—about Israel and Palestine, but also about history and many social and political issues, from the environment to gender to capitalism. Indeed, it's impossible to understand progressive politics today without grasping the idea of settler colonialism and the worldview that derives from it.

While no one could mistake the extremely negative connotation of the term *settler colonial* in the pro-Hamas statements, its exact meaning isn't self-evident, especially since both of its components are often used in a more neutral, descriptive fashion. In the context of Israel and Palestine, the word *settler* commonly refers to Jews living on territory occupied by Israel in the Six-Day War in 1967. In 2020 there were about 450,000 Jews living in West Bank settlements, out of a total Israeli Jewish population of nearly 7 million.

These settlements are outside the internationally recognized borders of Israel, the so-called Green Line determined by the armistice that ended the country's war of independence in 1949. Because they are widely considered illegal under international law and present a major obstacle to the creation of any future Palestinian state, they are condemned around the world. In Israel, too, they are controversial: according to a 2016 Pew report, Israeli Jews who identified themselves as on the political left "overwhelmingly say settlements hurt Israel's security," while those on the right say the opposite.[6]

The Israelis killed on October 7 were not settlers in this sense. They lived in small communities in the southern part of the country, inside the Green Line, near the border with the Gaza Strip. Referring to these places as "settler colonies" means abolishing the usual distinction between Israeli settlers living on occupied territory and citizens of Israel living inside their own country. All Israeli Jews, on this view, belong to the category of illegitimate settlers, because Israel itself is a settler colonial state.

Ironically, this understanding is identical with that of the religious nationalists who build outposts in the West Bank, only with the value judgment reversed. Those nationalist settlers agree that there is no meaningful distinction between Israel and the Occupied Territories. The difference is that they believe all of historic Palestine "between the river and the sea" belongs to Israel, while foes of settler colonialism believe that none of it does.

The word *colonial*, too, changes meaning when it enters into the compound *settler colonial*. Here the most important context is American history, which informs the concept of settler colonialism even more than Israel's. In the United

States, the period from the early 1600s to the American Revolution is known as the colonial era, when British settlers crossed the Atlantic and created the original thirteen colonies. This period ended when American colonists threw off their allegiance to Britain and declared, in the words of the Declaration of Independence, that "these United Colonies are, and of Right ought to be Free and Independent States." People who came to the United States after independence, down to the present day, are not called colonists but immigrants.

When theorists and activists describe America as a colonial society, however, they are referring not to the eighteenth century but to the twenty-first. As historian Adam Dahl writes, "'Colonial America' names not a phase of American intellectual and political development, but the settler colonial foundations of American democracy that continue to structure the basic features of modern democratic thought and politics."[7] In other words, the United States is a settler colonial society not because it was once a group of colonies under British rule, but because it is a colonial power, illegitimately occupying land that rightfully belongs to Native Americans—and always will.

The most frequently quoted sentence in the literature of settler colonialism, from the Australian scholar Patrick Wolfe, is "Invasion is a structure, not an event." Wolfe was referring specifically to the British settlement of Australia, but the principle applies equally to the United States and Canada, which were also created by dispossessing the peoples living there when Europeans arrived. This history is hardly unknown—everyone who grows up in these countries learns about it in elementary school.

What is new about settler colonialism is the idea that this original injustice is being renewed at every moment through various forms of oppression, some obvious, others invisible. Because settlement is not a past event but a present structure, every inhabitant of a settler colonial society who is not descended from the original indigenous population is, and always will be, a settler. "Understanding settler-colonialism means understanding that all non-Indigenous people are settler-colonizers, whether they were born here or not," explains the Southern Poverty Law Center (SPLC) in a primer on the subject.[8]

Settler, in this view, is not a description of the actions of an individual but a heritable identity. In fact, it's not even necessary to be the lineal descendant of an original dispossessor to qualify as a settler. Because settler colonialism is a structure, every nonindigenous person who occupies a place in that structure plays the role of settler, whether their ancestors arrived on the *Mayflower* or on a flight to LAX. "The social form of the American settler state foments an identification with settler ways of being," Jeffrey Sacks writes.[9] Even African Americans whose ancestors were brought to America in bondage "benefit from the settler-colonial system as it stands today," notes the SPLC.[10]

For the field called settler colonial studies, the goal of learning about settlement in America and elsewhere is not to understand it, as a historian would, but to combat it. "Making sense of how [settler colonial regimes] emerged and developed, and how settler colonial processes connect to others—such as capitalism, imperialism, racism, sexism, nationalism—must also mean setting out to think through how these structures of domination can be dismantled," insists Sai Englert of Leiden University.[11] "Protests, marches and sit-ins are forms of pedagogy," agrees Leigh Patel of the University of Pittsburgh School of Education, whose book on settler colonialism is titled *No Study Without Struggle*. These kinds of teaching are "not carried out for the sake of awarding grades but rather, in the interest of shifting mindsets and material realities."[12]

In the last two decades, settler colonial studies has become a flourishing academic discipline with its own scholarly journal. Hundreds of books and thousands of papers have been written on the subject, and it features in a wide range of college courses in the United States— not just on American history or Israel/Palestine, but on "Settler Colonial Ways of Seeing," "The Settler Colonial Determinants of Health," and "Native Feminisms and Settler Colonialism," to give just a few examples.

The concept is so fertile because it offers a political theory of original sin. Settler colonialism means that the violence involved in a nation's founding continues to define every aspect of its life, even after centuries—its economic arrangements, environmental practices, gender relations. The only way for a society to purge that sin is to decolonize,

and the increasing currency of this term is an index of the
rising influence of what might seem a recondite academic
idea. The command to "decolonize" has become almost
faddish; guides have been written on how to decolonize
your diet, your bookshelf, your backyard, your corporate
board, and much more.

Another expression of this impulse is land acknowledgments, in which institutions like universities and museums
formally declare that they stand on land once occupied by
a Native American tribe. First popularized in Australia
and Canada, land acknowledgments have become ubiquitous in the United States in recent years. Baylor University, for instance, offers this formula to be recited at official
events: "We respectfully acknowledge that Baylor University in Waco and its original campus in Independence are
on the land and territories originally occupied by Indigenous peoples including the Waco and Tawakoni of the
Wichita and Affiliate Tribes, the Tonkawa, the N~~umunu~~u
(Comanche), Karankawa, and Lipan Apache. These Indigenous peoples were dispossessed of and removed from their
lands over centuries by European colonization and American expansionism."

It would be strange if the purpose of land acknowledgments were simply to remind people of a fact that everyone
already knows—that the United States exists on land once
controlled by Native Americans. Rather, these formulas
serve to ritually renew the audience's responsibility for the
act of dispossession, in accordance with the settler colonial

view of history. The institution making the acknowledgment affirms its virtue by confirming its guilt.

How one might go about actually "decolonizing" the United States is, as we shall see, difficult to specify or even imagine. But settler colonial studies often speaks of the importance of interrupting, dismantling, and refusing "settler futures"—that is, futures in which settler colonial societies like the United States and Israel continue to exist. In one of the field's most influential papers, "Decolonization Is Not a Metaphor," Eve Tuck of SUNY New Paltz and K. Wayne Yang of UC San Diego write that "relinquishing settler futurity" is necessary if we are to imagine "the Native futures, the lives to be lived once the settler nation is gone."[13]

On October 7, Hamas did more than imagine it. By killing old people and children inside the borders of Israel, it acted on the principle that every citizen of a settler colonial state is a fair target, because none of them has a right to be there. For many critics of settler colonialism whose opposition consisted merely of theory and invective, this highly concrete interruption of settler futures was—as one Cornell professor told a student rally—"exhilarating" and "energizing."[14]

It may seem paradoxical that opposing what one scholar calls "the slow violence of settler colonialism" should lead people to celebrate the quick violence of terrorism.[15] But part of the appeal of radical ideologies, of the right and the left, is that they make violence virtuous. And October 7 marked the moment when settler colonialism emerged into public view as the watchword of a new ideology, one that is already influencing the way many Americans think about their country and the world.

One sign that this worldview hasn't fully emerged as a self-conscious movement is that it has no agreed-upon name. To call it the ideology of settler colonialism is potentially misleading, since it means naming a political idea after what it opposes. Moreover, within settler colonial studies, terms like *settler ideology* are used to refer to the ideas by which settler colonial regimes sustain their own domination. Still, it makes sense to speak about the ideology of settler colonialism, because the term itself is highly ideological, aiming to shape our sense of reality in accordance with a particular interpretation of politics and history.

Like other radical ideologies, this one can be difficult to oppose because it is rooted in a praiseworthy moral instinct: indignation against injustice. European settlement of the Americas destroyed the lives and cultures of millions of indigenous people, and their surviving descendants continue to suffer materially and spiritually as a result. Hundreds of thousands of Palestinian Arabs were driven from their homes in Israel's war of independence, and Palestinians living under Israeli occupation continue to suffer today.

Unfortunately, indignation against past injustice is not a sufficient basis for remedying it. On the contrary, history shows that it can easily become the source of new injustices. In exploring the ideology of settler colonialism, we will see that it falls into many of the errors to which radical ideologies are traditionally prone. It attributes many different varieties of injustice to the same abstraction and promises that slaying this dragon will end them all. It cultivates hatred for people and institutions it sees as obstacles to redemption, and even justifies violence against them. And it offers a distorted account of history, to make it easier to divide the world into the guilty and the innocent. These ways of thinking have traditionally produced disastrous results, and the ideology of settler colonialism is already leading idealistic, educated young people down a similar path. That makes it urgent to understand where the idea comes from and where it is likely to lead.

2

Redefining Colonialism

Today the term *settler colonialism* is used to describe the political and social regime in countries like the United States, Australia, and Canada, where European settlers replaced indigenous peoples over generations of war and dispossession. But this is a relatively recent transformation of a concept that once meant something significantly different. Tracing that shift can help to clarify what today's theorists of settler colonialism mean by it, and the intellectual contradictions at its core.

The story begins in the mid-twentieth century, when the world began to reckon with European colonialism and its malign legacies. At the end of World War II, the victorious Allies stripped the Axis powers of the territories they had conquered—Germany in Central and Eastern Europe, Japan in East and Southeast Asia. Reversing these conquests wasn't only a matter of punishing the defeated. The right of all peoples to self-determination had been central to the Allied cause from the beginning, when Britain and France went to war to defend the independence of Poland. In the Atlantic Charter drawn up by Franklin Roosevelt and Winston Churchill in August 1941, the leaders declared that one of their main war aims was to "respect the right of all peoples to choose the form of government under which they will live; and they wish to see sovereign rights and self-government restored to those who have been forcibly deprived of them."

Yet even after World War II, almost one-third of the world's population continued to live under forcibly imposed foreign rule—and their overlords, in most cases, were the very Allied powers that had just fought a war in the name of self-government. The British Empire reached its greatest extent in 1945, stretching from Burma and India in Southeast Asia, through Palestine and Egypt in the Middle East, to Kenya, Nigeria, and Rhodesia in Africa. France ruled much of Indochina and North Africa, Belgium controlled the Congo, and the Netherlands was fighting to regain control of Indonesia. But the war had exhausted the economic resources and political will needed to sustain these empires, and in the two decades after 1945, they would be almost completely dismantled. According to the UN, the number of people living under colonial rule fell from 750 million in 1945 to 2 million in 2020.[1]

Decolonization was not as violent as colonialism itself,

but it was nowhere a peaceful process. Even where the imperial power withdrew voluntarily, liberated peoples often went to war to determine the borders of the successor states, as in India and Israel. When imperial powers resisted decolonization, they succeeded only in making the process longer and bloodier. The French fought from 1946 to 1954 to keep control over Vietnam, without success. A few months later Algeria rebelled against French rule, and another long colonial war began, ending with Algerian independence in 1962.

In addition to changing the map of the world, the decolonization struggle sparked an intellectual revolution. For centuries, European imperialism had been sustained by an ideological belief in the superiority of the West. In the 1950s and '60s, activists and thinkers across Asia, Africa, and the Middle East set out to demolish this intellectual legacy, in part by analyzing the complex relationship between the colonizer and the colonized.

The concept of settler colonialism was a product of this effort to understand the different forms of colonial rule. India, for instance, was part of the British Empire for almost two hundred years, starting in the mid-eighteenth century, but the number of Britons who lived in the subcontinent was very small. A 1931 census found a total of about 150,000 "European British subjects" in all of what is now India and Pakistan, out of a total population of more than 250 million. Similarly, on the eve of World War II, about 40,000 Frenchmen ruled about 23 million Vietnamese.

In these colonies, almost all the Europeans were military, commercial, and administrative personnel who came for a period and then returned home. Their goal was to extract profit, not to occupy the land.

In other colonies, however, Europeans did settle in significant numbers. After the British added South Africa to their empire in the early nineteenth century, many Britons emigrated there, joining the Boers, who had settled earlier under Dutch rule. By 1918, the South African census recorded a white population of about 1.4 million, out of 7 million total. On the other end of the continent, French Algeria was governed not as a colony but an integral part of France, and Europeans were given incentives to settle there. By the time Algeria won its independence in 1962, its population of about 10 million was 15 percent European.

In countries like these, the process of decolonization was bound to be much more complicated. European settlers exerted strong pressure on the imperial power to stay, fearing what would happen if they were left on their own. In Algeria, when the settlers known as *pieds noirs* feared they might be abandoned, they launched a successful coup to bring down France's Fourth Republic. In the British colony of Rhodesia, where whites made up 8 percent of the population, Prime Minister Ian Smith tried to avert Black majority rule by preemptively declaring independence in 1965, then spent the next decade and a half fighting a civil war.

In the 1970s, social scientists began to explore the

unique dynamics of decolonization in such places. One of the first to describe them as "settler colonial" societies was Kenneth Good, an Australian-born political scientist who taught briefly at the University of Rhodesia, before he was expelled from the country for opposing Smith's government. In 1976 Good published a scholarly article on "Settler Colonialism: Economic Development and Class Formation," in which he observed that colonies where Europeans had settled in significant numbers, including Rhodesia, Algeria, and South Africa, had followed a different path than the rest.[2]

The standard explanation of European imperialism held that expanding capitalist societies needed colonies "as perpetual suppliers of raw materials, and as providers of dependent domestic markets," Good wrote. This role relegated colonies to the "periphery" of the world economy, and after independence they were plagued by "underdevelopment and dependency."

But countries shaped by European settlement had a different economic structure. Thanks to their "heavy exploitation of African land and labor," these colonies developed more advanced capitalist economies, in which the native population functioned as a proletariat. Good argued, along Marxist lines, that this exploitation "inadvertently" created a more self-conscious and dynamic African working class that acquired "skills and organization for change, born of the needs and resources of the capitalist economy." For this reason he predicted, correctly, that apartheid rule in Rhodesia and South Africa could not survive for long. Paradoxically, Good concluded, "economic development produc[es] a capacity for revolutionary class action which renders settler colonialism dangerous to imperialism."

In light of the later development of the term *settler colonialism*, two things about Good's understanding of the concept are especially significant. First, for him, it wasn't a purely negative phenomenon. Rather, like capitalism in Marx's theory of class conflict, it played a paradoxical double role, accelerating historical progress even as it created misery.

Second, Good used *settler colonialism* to describe the handful of African countries where a small population of white settlers dominated a much larger native population. He did not think of applying the label to countries like the United States, Canada, and Australia, where European settlement began much earlier, in the seventeenth and eighteenth centuries, and most of the indigenous population was displaced or destroyed by war and disease. Good's revolutionary optimism about Rhodesia and South Africa could not be applied to countries where there was no class-conscious, numerically superior native population preparing to challenge white rule.

In the 1980s and '90s, however, the definition of settler colonialism underwent a crucial shift as Australian theorists began to apply the term to their own country, even though it did not meet the traditional definition of a colony. Unlike French Algeria, Australia was not governed by its mother country, maintaining merely formal ties to Great Britain through the British Commonwealth. And unlike South Africa, there was no settler class ruling over a native population. Rather, in Australia as in the United States, a white, European-descended population had largely replaced indigenous peoples.

So when anthropologist Patrick Wolfe applied the term *settler colonialism* to Australia, in his influential 1999 book *Settler Colonialism and the Transformation of Anthropology*, he was defining it in a new way.[3] The book's primary subject is the academic discipline of anthropology and its "ideological entanglements" with Aboriginal culture. But its influence is owed less to Wolfe's analysis of anthropological theory than to his attack on "Australian settler colonialism," especially in the introduction.

For Wolfe, unlike for Good, this form of society is not defined by a settler class exploiting indigenous labor. Rather, he argues that the creation of settler colonies required clearing the land for a new society, which meant getting rid of the people already living there. This could mean killing or expelling indigenous people, but it could also mean destroying their culture and peoplehood, then absorbing the remnants into the new society constructed on the ruins. "Settler colonies were not primarily established to extract surplus value from indigenous labor," Wolfe writes. "Rather, they are premised on displacing indigenes from (or replacing them on) the land."

In this new definition, settler colonies are precisely those countries—like Australia, Canada, and the United

States—where people do *not* think of themselves as settlers, because they have taken over the land so successfully that they see themselves as natives. Wolfe sums up his definition of settler colonialism in an often-quoted sentence: "The colonizers came to stay—invasion is a structure not an event."

The first part of this statement is a truism: Of course, colonies like Australia were established by Europeans who came (or were sent) to dwell permanently in a new land. Wolfe's innovation lies in the second part, which insists that the passage of time can never turn these invaders or their descendants into authentic inhabitants. He makes the same point when he writes, "Settler colonies were (are) premised on the elimination of native societies." The parenthesis implies that the elimination of native societies is not something that happened in the past—British settlement in Australia began in 1788, in North America in 1607—but something that is happening right now and will continue to happen as long as nonindigenous people remain on territory that can never be legitimately theirs.

When Wolfe's book was published, Australia was in the thick of the "history wars," a cultural and political debate that began among historians but soon drew in the public. At its core was the question of whether Australians should be proud or ashamed of their country's past, and in particular, whether white settlement constituted a genocide of the continent's indigenous people. To conservatives who held a patriotic view of Australian history, progressive revisionists were the "black armband" school, since they wanted Australians to be forever in mourning for the crimes of the past. Progressives retorted that the conservatives had a "white blindfold" approach, refusing to see the ugly truth.

Wolfe's book, while highly specialized, was unmistakably an intervention in this debate, and his definition of settler colonialism can be seen as the most uncompromising statement of the "black armband" position. He was not the first person to describe colonialism as a genocidal enterprise. After World War II, the German Jewish philosopher Hannah Arendt argued in *The Origins of Totalitarianism* that important features of the Nazi regime, including ideological racism and bureaucratic lawlessness, were pioneered by colonial regimes in Africa before being brought home to Europe. Aimé Césaire, the Martinican poet and politician, wrote that Europeans "tolerated Nazism before it was inflicted on them, that they absolved it, shut their eyes to it, legitimized it, because, until then, it had been applied only to non-European peoples."[4] Arendt would have disagreed with that equivalence; she believed that the "experience of concentration camps and death factories" was "remote" from imperialism, whose "horrors were still marked by a certain moderation." But at least both thinkers agreed that the horror of colonialism was its horrors—killing, enslavement, racism.

What is distinctive about the ideology of settler colonialism is that it proposes a new syllogism: if settlement is a genocidal invasion, and invasion is an ongoing structure, not a completed event, then everything (and perhaps everyone) that sustains a settler colonial society today is also genocidal. As Wolfe put it in his seminal 2006 paper "Settler Colonialism and the Elimination of the Native," "logic that initially informed frontier killing transmutes into different modalities, discourses and institutional formations as it undergirds the historical development and complexification of settler society."[5]

This sentence can be seen as a mission statement for the academic discipline of settler colonial studies. Not all the research and writing carried out under that rubric is directly ideological or aims to inform current political debates. In the introduction to *The Routledge Handbook of the History of Settler Colonialism*, the Australian theorist Lorenzo Veracini writes that "settler colonialism has no geographical, cultural or chronological bounds,"[6] and historians have applied the concept to a wide range of historical phenomena, from ancient Greek city-states to the Japanese conquest of Manchuria in the 1930s. But in practice, settler colonial studies is usually concerned with the countries where it has flourished as an academic discipline—Australia, Canada, and the United States. Its other major focus, as we shall see, is Israel, despite the enormous difference in historical experience between the Jewish state and the Anglophone countries.

If settler colonial studies aspired to be a true historical discipline, its narrow limits would be disqualifying. They make perfect sense, however, if it is understood as a variety of critical theory, directed at what Wolfe called the "discourses and institutional formations" responsible for social injustice in Western countries. The original critical theory, developed by mid-twentieth-century German thinkers like Theodor Adorno and Max Horkheimer, analyzed that injustice in Marxist terms. The critical race theory that emerged in American law schools in the 1970s understood it in terms of racism. Today, settler colonial studies understands it as the legacy—better, the persistence—of a founding genocide. As Wolfe writes, "The question of genocide is never far from discussions of settler colonialism."[7]

The word *genocide* was coined in 1944 by Raphael Lemkin, a Polish Jewish lawyer who fled Nazism and ended up working for the War Department in Washington, D.C. In his study *Axis Rule in Occupied Europe*, Lemkin used the term to describe the Nazi extermination of Jews, which had not yet been named the Holocaust or the Shoah. "New conceptions require new terms. By 'genocide' we mean the destruction of a nation or of an ethnic group," he wrote, explaining that the word combines "the ancient Greek word *genos* (race, tribe) and the Latin *cide* (killing)."[8]

Ever since, the Holocaust has been the paradigmatic genocide. The term was later applied to mass murders that resembled it in scale, such as the killing of 2 million Cambodians by the Khmer Rouge in the late 1970s, and the massacre of 800,000 Tutsis in Rwanda in 1994. But settler colonial studies defines genocide much more broadly. In fact, Damien Short of the University of London argues that "it isn't actually necessary for anyone to be killed in order for genocide to take place." For Lemkin, the essence of the crime was "the destruction of essential foundations of the life of national groups"; killing all the individual members of a group was only the means to that end.

It follows, according to Short, that "we should view cultural genocide as central to our understanding of genocide itself. By extension I argue that the concept is an appropriate term to describe the current experiences of many indigenous peoples living under settler colonial rule."[9] Short believes that "industrial mining and farming" and "even national park schemes" should be considered part of the "genocide machine" that sustains settler colonialism, because they maintain control over land that once belonged to indigenous peoples.

No one has done more to expand the definition of genocide in settler colonial studies than Veracini, who teaches at Australia's Swinburne University of Technology and cofounded the journal *Settler Colonial Studies*. For Veracini, mass murder is just one expression of what he calls the "transferist imagination" of settler colonialism, since transferring an indigenous population out of its native place can take many forms other than outright elimination.[10] In his book *Settler Colonialism: A Theoretical Overview*, Veracini offers a taxonomy in which "necropolitical transfer"—"when the indigenous communities are militarily liquidated"—is just the first of twenty-six varieties of transfer, listed from A to Z.

With the exception of necropolitical transfer and the next on the list, "ethnic transfer"—forcible deportation of an entire ethnic group—none of these involve physical elimination. "Transfer by assimilation," for instance, is the exact opposite of removal: it means incorporating indigenous people into the settler society, for instance by making them citizens, which metaphorically "raises" them out of their native place onto a supposedly higher plane of civilization.

An indigenous people can also be "discursively" transferred by denying that it really belongs on the settler's territory. For instance, Veracini argues that referring to Algerians and Palestinians as Arabs is transferist, because it implies that they are part of a larger collective that inhabits many places, rather than belonging exclusively to Algeria or Palestine. (Presumably it doesn't negate the point that these peoples refer to themselves as Arabs: Hamas's 2017 declaration of "Principles and Policies" begins, "Palestine is the land of the Arab Palestinian people.")

In "multicultural transfer," meanwhile, indigenous people lose their unique status as the original possessors of the land and become just another of the nation's ethnic minorities. And in "transfer by performance," Veracini writes, "settlers dress up as natives," as in the Boston Tea Party; in doing so, they "occupy native identities," metaphorically evicting the rightful owners.

It is not strictly necessary, of course, for Veracini's list to include exactly as many items as there are letters in the alphabet. The purpose of the A to Z taxonomy is to condemn every possible relationship between settler and native. Inclusion and exclusion, imitation and rejection, public acknowledgment and official erasure—all are varieties of transfer, all participate in the logic of genocide. Even "reconciliation" between settlers and natives contributes to "the extinction of otherwise irreducible forms of indigenous alterity." In the end, Veracini concludes, "no matter how much it tries, the settler colonial situation cannot ultimately supersede itself."

Indeed, because settler colonialism is such a comprehensive crime, extending hundreds of years into the past and embracing every facet of society, it is very difficult to imagine how it might be overcome, or even what it would mean to overcome it. This makes the struggle against settler colonialism essentially different from other progressive causes. The slogan "pessimism of the intellect, optimism of the will," used by the Italian Marxist thinker Antonio Gramsci in interwar Europe, is a favorite of radicals faced with the failure of utopian hopes; today it's often heard from climate activists. The formula suggests that a revolutionary must have a realistic notion of how difficult it is to achieve victory, while never ceasing to believe that victory is possible.

Writers on settler colonialism ritually affirm that its legacy must be overthrown, but it is hard for them to summon any real optimism of the will—not simply because the road ahead looks difficult, but because it's hard to say where that road goes. Even if a settler colonial nation issues an apology for its past treatment of indigenous people, Veracini notes, there is "no compelling or intuitively acceptable story about what should happen *next*."

This dead end became unavoidable the moment settler colonialism was redefined to describe countries like the United States and Australia, rather than countries like Algeria and Rhodesia. In the latter, the goals of decolonization were clear: national independence and the seizure of power, and perhaps property as well, from the settler class. But in the former, the people described as settlers are almost the entire population; in 2021, only 3 percent of Australia's population of 25 million was Aboriginal. And these settlers can't go back home, because they have no mother country beside the one they are living in.

One alternative would be for settler colonial societies to cede part of their territory and sovereignty to indigenous peoples. This would not be a form of reparation for past crimes, the way Germany awarded money to Holocaust survivors, but a recognition that the settler state's acquisition of native land was null and void from the start. "Native title does not inhere in Indigenous people because the Australian government deigned to concede it to them," Wolfe writes. "On the contrary, their title predates and is independent of the institutions that Europeans brought to Australia."[11]

Tuck and Yang reach a similar conclusion about the United States: "Decolonization eliminates settler property

rights and settler sovereignty. It requires the abolition of
land as property and upholds the sovereignty of Native
land and people." In practice, this would mean "repatriat-
ing land to sovereign Native tribes and nations," though
Tuck and Yang, like all other theorists of settler colonialism, fail to specify what parts of the United States should
be returned to which Native tribes, or what would happen
to the people living there. "Decolonization is not obliged
to answer those questions," they declare, because "decolonization is not accountable to settlers, or settler futurity.
Decolonization is accountable to Indigenous sovereignty
and futurity."[12]

If the definition of a progressive movement is that it
believes the future can be better than the past, then the
ideology of settler colonialism is not progressive, because
it believes the past was better than the future. Its impossible goal is to turn the clock back to the world that existed
before 1788 or 1607 or 1492. "Settler colonization can be
visually understood as the unbroken pace of invasion, and
settler occupation, into Native lands," write Tuck and Yang.
"Decolonization, as a process, would repatriate land to
Indigenous peoples, reversing the timeline of these images."

Tuck and Yang refer to this backward turn as "relinquishing settler futurity," and they are impatient with any
evasion of the fact that decolonization is a zero-sum game,
in which Natives win (land, sovereignty, power) only if
settlers lose. Since, in twenty-first century America, less

than 3 percent of the population is Native American, this means that the premise of decolonization is exactly the reverse of the Occupy movement, which rallied the American left in the early 2010s by claiming to represent 99 percent of the people against the wealthiest 1 percent. "For social justice movements, like Occupy, to truly aspire to decolonization non-metaphorically, they would impoverish, not enrich, the 99%+ settler population of U.S.," Tuck and Yang insist (slightly underestimating the Native population).

This math makes decolonizing North America a radically different proposition from decolonizing Asia and Africa. From the Viet Minh in Vietnam to the Front de libération nationale (FLN) in Algeria, successful anticolonial movements united the vast majority of the population against a small class of settlers. In *The Wretched of the Earth*, his fiery 1961 polemic on behalf of decolonization, Frantz Fanon described Algeria's independence movement as "the people in arms," pointedly using a term invented during the French Revolution to legitimize a struggle against France. It's a reminder that modern revolutionary movements have usually been democratic in principle, even if their effects were not, because they spoke in the name of the many against the few. In the French Revolution, the people were many and the aristocrats were few; in the Russian Revolution, the poor were many and the rich were few.

The struggle against settler colonialism, by contrast, indicts the many in pursuit of justice for the few. In this respect, it resembles today's identitarian social justice movements, which confront the American majority with demands for inclusion and equality for minority groups. Since the 1960s, these movements have greatly improved American society. But the ideology of settler colonialism carries its oppositional stance to the breaking point by making a demand that cannot be satisfied even in principle, since the only way to undo the wrongs of settlement would be for America never to have existed.

This counterfactual aspiration removes the ideology of settler colonialism from the realm of politics, which helps explain why it has only a limited appeal to the people it claims to vindicate—Native Americans. Mainstream advocacy groups like the National Congress of American Indians and the Native American Rights Fund do not use the language of settler colonialism or name decolonization as one of their aims. Instead, they talk about defending tribal rights, enforcing treaties, and holding government accountable—concrete goals that can be achieved within the framework of American law.

Indeed, theorists of settler colonialism sometimes express impatience at the failure of Native Americans to follow their lead. "How can it be," demands Mahmood Mamdani of Columbia University, a prominent figure in settler colonial studies, "that even Indian activists, tribal governments, human rights tribunals, and scholars of indigeneity fail to see that the colonial relationship endures?"[13] His answer is that the victims of colonialism are also "formed by their embrace of it. To say so is not to blame the victim but to recognize that victims sometimes must go to terrible lengths to survive." For instance, Mamdani writes that Native Americans who believe in the importance of belonging to a tribe have fallen for a "racist notion . . . introduced by settlers" and embraced by "Indian rights activists claiming to preserve indigenous traditions."

Settler colonial studies does include Native activists and scholars, but it is mainly an academic enterprise, and in 2021 Native Americans made up less than one half of one percent of university professors.[14] Ijeoma Nnodim Opara, a physician and professor of public health at Wayne State University, has decried "the rush of Euro-American do-gooders to institutionalize decolonization centers, departments, positions, apply for grants, and create programs, projects, and curricula," characterizing this as an attempt to "colonize the decolonization movement."[15]

Writing about Australia's history wars in 2003, the historian Fiona Paisley observed that they "are not about Aboriginal history at all, but about a growing crisis in white identity in Australia."[16] A similar point can be made about the discourse of settler colonialism in the United States. It is primarily a conversation among "settlers" about their own identity, and what it offers is less a program for action than a political theology.

Ironically, it has clear parallels with the Calvinist

theology of predestination that inspired the first New England settlers, the Puritans, long ago in colonial Massachusetts. A settler colonial society "cannot supersede itself" in the same way that a Puritan could not extricate himself from the original sin he incurred before he was born. It might seem that this would make chastising the sinner pointless, but in fact the opposite is the case. For the Puritans, it was urgently necessary to bring people to an understanding of their fallenness, since it is only after embracing guilt that the workings of grace can begin.

The ideology of settler colonialism thrives on a similar paradox. By insisting that settler colonial societies are guilty of an irredeemable crime, it validates the most extreme criticism and denunciation of those societies, as long as it can be cast in the language of decolonization. The goal is not to change this or that public policy but to engender a permanent disaffection, a sense that the social order ought not to exist. One of the most potent ways to do this is to teach Americans a new way of thinking about the history of their country.

3

A New American Countermyth

Until relatively recently, Americans were educated to believe that the creation of the United States was a great and providential event. More was at stake in American history than America itself; as the first nation "conceived in liberty, and dedicated to the proposition that all men are created equal," in Abraham Lincoln's famous words, it was a test of the human capacity for self-government. Joel Barlow, a radical Jeffersonian writer and politician, gave expression to this idea in his 1807 epic *The Columbiad*, a *Paradise Lost*–style retelling of the discovery of America. For Barlow, the New World was where humanity would perfect itself:

But when he steps on these regenerate shores,
His mind unfolding for superior powers,

FREEDOM, his new Prometheus, here shall rise,
Light her new torch in my refulgent skies,
Touch with a stronger life his opening soul,
Of moral systems fix the central goal.

Barlow was a poet, but early American historians were hardly less rhapsodic. George Bancroft, who took decades to complete his monumental *History of the United States*, described his country as the culmination of human history to date: "Successions of increasing culture and heroes in the world of thought had conquered for mankind the idea of the freedom of the individual; the creative but long latent energy that resides in the collective reason was next to be revealed. From this the state was to emerge, like the fabled spirit of beauty and love out of the foam of the ever-troubled ocean."

This understanding of American history could be credible, even as a myth, only so long as the country was defined solely by the experience of its white citizens. Of course, writers like Barlow and Bancroft knew that the land of freedom was built in part by enslaved people from Africa, on territory conquered from Native Americans. But until the mid-twentieth century, at least, these parts of the American story were tacitly agreed, by the official tellers of that story, to be inessential. That was the price of sustaining the belief that the history of America was synonymous with the history of liberty.

Only after World War II, with the rise of the civil rights

movement, did the United States begin to grapple in earnest with the problem of reconciling patriotic myth with historical fact. As in Britain and France, the fight against Nazi racism and imperialism had made it difficult for Americans to ignore their own participation in those same evils. Indeed, many Black thinkers of the 1950s and '60s saw the civil rights movement as the American equivalent of the decolonization movements then sweeping Africa and Asia.

One of Martin Luther King's favorite sayings was "the arc of the moral universe is long but it bends toward justice"; many Americans know it from the speech he delivered in Selma, Alabama, in 1965. Eight years earlier he invoked the same idea after attending the independence ceremony for Ghana, formerly the British colony of Gold Coast. "Ghana tells us that the forces of the universe are on the side of justice," King told his congregation back home in Montgomery, Alabama. "An old order of colonialism, of segregation, discrimination is passing away now. And a new order of justice, freedom and good will is being born."

But the old order in the United States could not be fought in the same way as the old order in Ghana, where the British packed up and went home. One of King's most effective strategies was to develop a new understanding of American history that didn't completely repudiate the traditional one. Instead of insisting that the myth of American freedom was hypocritical and false, King suggested that it was incomplete. At the March on Washington, he compared the "magnificent words of the Constitution and the Declaration of Independence" to a promissory note that, for Black Americans, had never been paid. The goal of the civil rights movement was to force the United States to make good on its promises, to pay its debt. With this metaphor, King recast America's historical failure as an opportunity. By finally achieving racial equality, the United States could become the country it had always claimed to be.

This new version of the American story was so compelling that, in the half-century after King was murdered, it was embraced by politicians of all stripes. In a Martin Luther King Day speech in 2006, President George W. Bush declared, "At the dawn of this new century, America can be proud of the progress we have made toward equality, but we all must recognize we have more to do." When President Barack Obama dedicated Washington, D.C.'s King Memorial five years later, he said the same thing: "Nearly 50 years after the March on Washington, our work, Dr. King's work, is not yet complete." Of course, acknowledging that America's debt remains unpaid is not the same thing as helping to pay it, and many politicians have repeated King's idea without his insistence on "the fierce urgency of now." But binding the American establishment to this interpretation of history helped secure the gains of the civil rights movement.

One of the goals of the ideology of settler colonialism is to discredit this hopeful narrative. For the metaphor of America's unpaid debt works only if a creditor wants that debt to be paid—that is, if their demand is full inclusion in American society. "There will be neither rest nor tranquility in America until the Negro is granted his citizenship rights," King said in Washington. But from the point of view of settler colonialism, extending citizenship rights to Native Americans doesn't just fail to compensate for the original crime of colonization. It actually compounds that crime, by suggesting that it is no longer possible for Native Americans to define themselves outside the settler order. "From this point of view, a struggle for equal citizenship looks like a masked acceptance of final defeat: total colonization," writes Mamdani.[1]

For Veracini, citizenship is a case of "transfer by assimilation." He gives as an example Canada's Gradual Enfranchisement Act of 1869, which provided for indigenous people to become Canadian citizens by renouncing their tribal membership. In the United States, the Indian Citizenship Act of 1924, which extended birthright citizenship to all Native Americans, divided opinion for this reason. In becoming American citizens, some tribes feared they would lose their status as sovereign nations. Almost a century later, in 2018, the Onondaga Nation stated that it had "never accepted the authority of the US to make Six Nations citizens become citizens of the US, as claimed in the Citizenship Act of 1924," calling the law an "unsolicited grant of citizenship."[2]

The difference between the language of civil rights and the language of decolonization is that the former aims to perfect America, while the latter rejects it. For this reason, the ideology of settler colonialism strongly resists drawing analogies between Native Americans and other oppressed or disadvantaged minorities. To subsume "colonization under the umbrella of racism . . . is an intellectual error with consequences," Mamdani writes. "Blacks have been governed by a regime of white supremacy, the struggle against which has been incorporated into the American sense of self—a fact demonstrated by the comfort with which racists cite King and other icons of civil rights. Indians, by contrast, have been governed by colonialism, which, if recognized, would destroy the American sense of self."[3]

When Black and Native aspirations are placed in opposition in this way, it follows that, in seeking equality with white Americans, Blacks are embracing the guilt of the settler. As Tuck and Yang put it, "the attainment of equal legal and cultural entitlements" for all ethnic groups in America "is actually an investment in settler colonialism. Indeed, even the ability to be a minority citizen in the settler nation means an option to become a brown settler."

Seen through the lens of settler colonialism, it makes little difference that Europeans came to the United States voluntarily while Africans were sold into slavery, since the end result is the same: both are now living where they don't belong. As Kyle Mays of UCLA summarizes this view, "Black people are either erasing Indigenous peoples, attempting to replace them, or are outright settlers."[4]

When "Black people claim that they are owed land because of their exploited labor," Mays explains, they assume that the land is properly America's to dispose of, which implies "that settler colonialism will continue and Native people don't have a future." One might say that African American demands for an equal share in American prosperity are the equivalent of asking to be cut in on a thief's haul.

Other ethnic groups, too, can find themselves unexpectedly translated from the category of oppressed to that of oppressor. Laura Pulido of the University of Oregon explains that settler colonialism "unsettles Chicanas/os' conception of themselves as colonized people by highlighting their role as colonizers."[5] For instance, Pulido writes, Hispanic activists in the American Southwest challenged their treatment as second-class newcomers by pointing out that they had deeper roots in the region than white Americans, using the slogan "We didn't cross the border, the border crossed us." But while Texas and California were Mexican before they were American, Mexico itself was part of the Spanish Empire, created by European colonizers. As Pulido notes, "Chicana/o activists have imagined their homeland on the territories of dispossessed people."

These complexities show why the grievances of settler colonialism can't be redressed in the framework of multiculturalism. Multiculturalism, or what the early twentieth-century American writer Horace Kallen called "cultural pluralism," was conceived as a progressive alternative to the old ideal of assimilation.[6] Rather than forcing immigrants to conform to the culture of the "dominant classes," Kallen argued in his 1915 essay "Democracy Versus the Melting Pot" that America should embrace the ideal of "multiplicity in unity," in which each ethnic group contributes to the greater good by maintaining its specific "emotional and voluntary life." Instead of a melting pot, he wanted the United States to imagine itself as an orchestra, in which every instrument's unique timbre contributes to the beauty of the symphony.

But this metaphor presupposes that the orchestra has the right to exist in the first place. From the perspective of settler colonialism, Native Americans aren't just another an instrument in the orchestra; they are more like the rightful owners of the land on which the concert hall stands. To do justice to them would mean putting the orchestra out of business.

Historian Roxanne Dunbar-Ortiz offers a comprehensive statement of this anti-liberal position in her book *Not "A Nation of Immigrants."*[7] As the title indicates, Dunbar-Ortiz takes aim at an idea that might seem as anodyne as King's "promissory note." The notion that America is a "nation of immigrants," she writes, was introduced in a 1958 book by the historian Arthur Schlesinger, Jr., and embraced by President John F. Kennedy. For these mid-century liberals, the idea was meant to demolish any snobbish distinction between America's WASP elite and more recent arrivals from Ireland or Italy or Poland. The Puritans on the *Mayflower* were immigrants just like the huddled masses at Ellis Island; no group had a better claim to the title of American than any other.

For Dunbar-Ortiz, however, the notion that America is a nation of immigrants is a myth invented for propaganda purposes during the Cold War. Faced with decolonization movements around the world and a Soviet rival that claimed to champion them, "U.S. ruling classes" created a "revisionist origin story" to cloak the country's true origins, which are settler colonial. Because invasion is a structure, not an event, everyone who comes to live in the United States, regardless of where they came from, is a settler, responsible for continuing the dispossession and genocide that began in the seventeenth century. Calling these newcomers immigrants is merely an alibi, Dunbar-Ortiz insists: "The desire to relieve the non-European migrant or descendants of enslaved Africans from responsibility is understandable but not sustainable if the settler-colonial foundation is to be eradicated."

By insisting that American institutions and the American way of life are the responsibility of settlers, not immigrants, Dunbar-Ortiz takes a progressive route to the same conclusion as some nativist thinkers. A quarter-century ago, the political scientist Samuel Huntington also attacked the idea that America is a nation of immigrants, and also insisted that American identity and institutions were the work of white Anglo-Saxon settlers. But where Dunbar-Ortiz believes that these institutions are so powerful that they turn subsequent immigrants into settlers,

Huntington had the opposite fear—that multicultural immigration would erode the settler legacy, which he saw in positive terms.

In a 2000 lecture, Huntington posited that "from the earliest time American identity has been defined in terms of the Anglo-Protestant culture, values, and institutions of the founding settlers, including individualism, liberty, the work ethic, the rule of law, private property, and hostility to concentrated power."[8] Until the late twentieth century, he argued, immigrants to the United States who were neither Anglo nor Protestant felt a strong pressure to assimilate to this culture. But the advent of multiculturalism, combined with a steep increase in immigration from Mexico, threatened to erode the Anglo-Protestant matrix of American success. "Mexican immigration," Huntington concluded, "is a unique, disturbing, and looming challenge to our cultural integrity, our national identity, and potentially to our future as a country."

Huntington's distrust of immigrants and Dunbar-Ortiz's distrust of settlers end up converging from opposite directions, not unlike the way religious Zionists and anti-Zionists converge in their views of Israel's occupied territories. It's a familiar ideological phenomenon: the right and the left have often united in disparaging the compromises of liberalism, which they see as weakly evasive. And it's no accident that the ideology of settler colonialism is flourishing today at the same time as right-wing populism. Both see our turbulent political moment as an opportunity to permanently change the way Americans think about their country. As Mamdani writes, "the challenge of decolonizing" is "stripping away the nation . . . as a locus of political identification and commitment."[9]

If the traditional view of American history was triumphalist and exclusionary, and the liberal view is complacent and dishonest, the ideology of settler colonialism offers a new way of telling the American story—as an unmitigated disaster. In a sense, today's historians of settler colonialism, both academic and popular, agree with their nineteenth-century predecessors that the European discovery of the Americas and the creation of the United States were the hinges on which world history turned. But according to their new countermyth, it was a turn toward damnation, not redemption. As Dunbar-Ortiz puts it, America is something that should not have happened: "It should not have happened that the great civilizations of the Western Hemisphere, the very *evidence* of the Western Hemisphere, were wantonly destroyed, the gradual progress of humanity interrupted and set upon a path of greed and destruction."[10]

The rise of settler colonial studies has provoked a wave of new scholarship about Native American history, including some of the highest quality. *The Rediscovery of America: Native Peoples and the Unmaking of U.S. History* by Ned Blackhawk, a Yale professor of history who is a member of a Shoshone Indian tribe, won the National Book Award for Nonfiction in 2023. *Unworthy Republic: The Dispossession of Native Americans and the Road to Indian Territory*, by Claudio

Saunt of the University of Georgia, won the Bancroft Prize
for American History in 2021.

As the titles of these books suggest, their purpose isn't
simply to retell the history of Native American dispossession. It is to change the way readers think about America—
"unmaking" it, rendering it "unworthy"—by making that
dispossession the defining American story. "U.S. history as
we currently know it does not account for the centrality of
Native Americans," Blackhawk writes, and since "histories of Native America provide the starkest contrast to the
American ideal," insistence on their centrality naturally
discredits that ideal.[11]

Blackhawk shows that conflict with Native Americans
shaped the development of American laws and institutions
in concrete ways. One cause of the American Revolution
was that Britain's interest in maintaining good relations
with Indian tribes collided with Americans' desire to keep
expanding west into Indian lands. After the Revolution,
the first treaties ratified under the new Constitution were
with Indian tribes, setting a precedent for the roles of the
president and Congress in foreign affairs.

At the same time, Native peoples and institutions were
reciprocally shaped by conflict. Blackhawk emphasizes
that this was not a matter of passively enduring aggression
but of actively changing in order to respond to it: "Native
nations across the Americas . . . responded to the cycles of
colonialism and shaped the continent's historical development." This process involved technological and economic

adaptation: "Raiders took weapons as spoils of war and plundered Indians who were allied with Europeans or had traded with them. They stole their metals, cloths and, if possible, guns. Increasingly, they took captives to trade in colonial slave markets."

And while the inexorable result of European and American expansion was Native dispossession, the stages of that process often empowered some peoples at the expense of others. In the sixteenth century, Spain expanded its empire in Mexico by resettling Native peoples, in what Blackhawk calls "a form of Indigenous settler colonialism in which Spain's Native allies aided in the dispossession of other Native nations and benefited from such service by receiving titles to their lands." The Iroquois Confederacy arose in the seventeenth century in what is now western New York and Quebec, initially in response to French expansion, and "came to control many aspects of the economic, social, and political affairs in eastern America during the 17th and much of the 18th century."

In telling the story of Native Americans in terms of power and agency, as well as dispossession and death, Blackhawk departs from the usual narrative of settler colonialism. As he writes in his introduction, "the field of settler colonial studies . . . often foregrounds Indigenous 'elimination' as the defining aspect of Native American history and minimizes the extent of Indigenous power and agency. It also struggles to assess changing power dynamics over time and leaves less space for recognizing Indigenous sovereignty across vast swaths of territories and over long periods. To build a new theory of American history will require recognizing that Native peoples simultaneously determined colonial economies, settlements, and politics and were shaped by them."

Another way of expressing this difference between history and settler colonial studies is that the former is primarily interested in the past, while the latter is primarily interested in using a story about the past to change the present. And for that purpose, it's necessary to make the past as morally legible as possible. One way of accomplishing this is to describe the violence of white settlers against Natives, while omitting any mention of the violence deployed by Natives resisting settler expansion.

In *An Indigenous Peoples' History of the United States*, for instance, Dunbar-Ortiz describes the Pequot War of 1636–38, in which Puritans and Pequot Indians fought for control of the Connecticut River Valley. She writes that "a single violent incident triggered a devastating Puritan war against the Pequots," in which "the Puritan settlers, as if by instinct, jumped immediately into a hideous war of annihilation, entering Indigenous villages and killing women and children or taking them hostage." But she does not say what this "incident" was or who committed the violence in question.

In his book on the Pequot War, historian Alfred Cave explains that the conflict began in July 1636 when an English trader named John Oldham was murdered by Natives on board his ship. The colonist who discovered Oldham's body said it was "stark naked, his head cleft to the brains, and his hands and legs cut as if they had been cutting them off."[12] Rather than "jumping immediately" into a war of annihilation, the Puritans spent months exchanging retaliatory raids with the Pequots, in which parties from each side burned enemy villages and killed civilians. The violence turned into a wider war after a Pequot raid on Wethersfield, Connecticut, in April 1637 killed nine settlers, prompting the colony of Connecticut to declare war in alliance with the Narragansetts, another Native people long at odds with the more powerful Pequots.

Almost a year of fighting culminated when Puritans and Narragansetts burned a Pequot village at Mystic, killing up to four hundred people. Dunbar-Ortiz quotes the notorious description of the massacre in William Bradford's *History of Plymouth Plantation*: "It was a fearful sight to see them thus frying in the fire, and the streams of blood quenching the same, and horrible was the stink and scent thereof, but the victory seemed a sweet sacrifice."

As this suggests, the Pequot War is a prime example of the way English settlers committed and sanctified violence against Native Americans. But it also shows how different Native peoples saw the arrival of European settlers as an opportunity as well as a threat, and how both sides came to feel that they were dealing with an inhuman, implacable enemy with whom there could be no peaceful coexistence. This historical complexity is invisible in Dunbar-Ortiz's account; her description of the settlers as instinctively and hideously violent is the mirror image of the way American historians used to write about Indians.

Conversely, the ideology of settler colonialism describes Native American life in idealized and ahistorical terms. Dunbar-Ortiz calls pre-Columbian North America a "relatively disease-free paradise" and a "comparative paradise of natural resources," where "wealthy peoples" lived "long and well with abundant ceremonial and recreational periods." Wars took place, but they hardly counted, since fighting was "highly ritualized, with quests for individual glory, resulting in few deaths."

This account inverts the traditional American belief in the unique savagery of Indian warfare; but turning a myth upside-down only produces a different myth. In their book *North American Indigenous Warfare and Ritual Violence*, scholars Richard Chacon and Ruben Mendoza write that among Native American peoples, "Warfare was ubiquitous; every major culture area of native North America . . . has produced archaeological, ethnohistorical, osteological, or ethnographic evidence of armed conflict and ritual violence."[13]

At one fourteenth-century cemetery in Illinois, "about 16 percent of several hundred burials showed signs of having died a violent death, with evidence of decapitation, scalping, blunt force trauma, and arrow points embedded in bone."[14] In western Alaska, Native warriors used tactics that sound very similar to those used by the Puritans at Mystic: "The objective was to catch everyone inside the buildings and block the doors. Torches and flammable material were then dropped into the buildings through the skylights. After the fire and smoke had had sufficient time to build up, the people inside the building had the alternatives of staying inside and suffocating or burning to death, or trying to escape and being clubbed or speared to death."[15]

The point of noting such facts is not to excuse the violence directed against Native Americans, which was more destructive over a longer period than the violence they could wield in response. It is to show that the account of American history offered by settler colonial studies is tailored to cultivate hostility to settlers.

In *Indigenous Continent*, a survey of Native resistance to European and American expansion, Finnish historian Pekka Hämäläinen makes even more tendentious generalizations. For instance, in the eleventh and twelfth centuries, a city now known as Cahokia flourished near present-day St. Louis. Based on surviving mounds and artifacts, it is believed to have been home to up to forty thousand people, making it the largest urban center in North America. The site was abandoned in the mid-fourteenth century, 150 years before Columbus, for unknown reasons—the civilization left no written records, and archaeologists have proposed a variety of explanations, including resource depletion, climate change, and invasion.

Hämäläinen, however, argues that the abandonment of Cahokia and other related settlements was "symptomatic" of the fact that people had found urban living, and the large-scale agriculture needed to support it, to be insufficiently egalitarian. "All across the eastern half of the continent," he writes, "people seem to have rejected the domineering priestly class for more collective and egalitarian social arrangements."[16] On this slender evidentiary basis, Hämäläinen concludes that what Europeans saw as Native Americans' "failure or aberration of civilization" was in fact a deliberate rejection of what Europeans meant by "civilization": "North American Indians had experimented with ranked societies and all-powerful spiritual leaders and had found them deficient and dangerous. They had opted for more horizontal, participatory, and egalitarian ways of being in the world—a communal ethos available to everyone who was capable of proper thoughts and deeds and willing to share their possessions." They achieved this enlightenment at the very moment that benighted medieval Europeans were falling into the trap of hierarchy: "common people fell under a select cadre of holy men who mobilized them to construct towering structures that glorified the otherworldly—and its servants on Earth."

If this fable about the virtue and selflessness of Native Americans sounds familiar, that is because it reiterates tropes that began to appear in Europe almost as soon as Columbus returned with news of a New World. In 1516, Thomas More's *Utopia* imagined a Spanish sailor discovering an island where "there is no unequal distribution, so that . . . no man has anything, yet they are all rich." More contrasts this frugal virtue with the love of money that fills Christendom with "frauds, thefts, robberies, quarrels, tumults, contentions, seditions, murders, treacheries, and witchcrafts." Two centuries later, in his poem *An Essay on Man*, Alexander Pope contrasted Christians, who "thirst for gold," with the "poor Indian," for whom "To be, contents his natural desire."

Settler colonial studies inherits this tradition of moralizing against Western vice by exalting Native virtue. Ironically, it recapitulates the very habits of mind it means to attack, imposing European and American categories on Native American life in a kind of discursive imperialism. A prime example is the custom of referring to North America as Turtle Island, ostensibly to reclaim an identity that existed before Columbus.

The name is inspired by an Iroquois creation myth, which says that the earth grew from mud placed on the shell of a turtle. Hämäläinen relates a version of the tale: "The water animals—the beaver, the loon, and many others—dived deep, trying to bring back mud from the bottom of the sea for Sky Woman to walk on, but they all failed. Only the Muskrat succeeded, delivering a handful of mud. The animals spread it on the Turtle's back and saw that the mud had the power to expand. It became an island, then an enormous expanse of dry land. That was the birthplace and home of the Iroquois people."

The practice of referring to North America as Turtle Island was largely inspired by the poet Gary Snyder, whose book *Turtle Island* won the Pulitzer Prize in 1975. In the introduction, Snyder writes, "The 'U.S.A.' and its states and counties are arbitrary and inaccurate impositions on what is really here," anticipating the central premise of settler colonial studies.[17] His poems contrast our polluted industrial civilization—"the rot at the heart / In the sick fat veins of Amerika"—with the pristine nature that existed before Europeans arrived.

Today the name Turtle Island is used as a kind of shorthand for the idea of American illegitimacy. Three weeks after the Hamas attack in Israel, Jaskiran Dhillon of the New School spoke at a pro-Palestine teach-in where she called the school "a university on Turtle Island" and referred to "the settler colony we know as the United States of America."[18]

The online *Canadian Encyclopedia* reports as a historical fact "settlers' renaming of Turtle Island to North America," calling it an example of "the Anglicization . . . of Indigenous place names and stories."[19] Yet the name Turtle Island is itself a product of "settler" ways of thinking, not Native ones. It turns one tribe's creation myth into a generic Native American concept, thus erasing the actual differences in belief between peoples. And it names a geographical entity—the continent of North America—that no Native people had any conception of before 1492, any more than Europeans did.

In fact, the encyclopedia's account has things exactly backward. The name America was not invented to change

the identity of a place previously called Turtle Island;
rather, the name Turtle Island was invented to change the
identity of the place called America. It tells us little about
what actually existed on this continent before 1492, but
a great deal about disaffection with the civilization that
exists here in the twenty-first century. In this sense, the
name Turtle Island perfectly encapsulates the ideology of
settler colonialism, which is less interested in the reality of
the past than in the construction of an alternative future.

4

Settler Ways of Being

Pekka Hämäläinen's *Indigenous Continent* ends with a reassurance that Native American peoples are bound to outlast the United States: "On an Indigenous timescale, the United States is a mere speck." But on the question of exactly how settler colonialism is to disappear, and what will take its place when it does, settler colonial studies tends to slip into evasive pieties. For Robin D. G. Kelley of UCLA, decolonization is "the space . . . where colonized people dream of liberation," "the memory/dreams/fantasy of life before and beyond invasion."[1] Englert writes that "Indigenous resistance" involves "maintaining memories of the worlds that were, as well as the worlds that can be."[2] For Tuck and Yang, "the lives to be lived once the settler nation is gone" are "unwritten possibilities."[3] And Patel predicts or warns that "decolonization and liberation, when we pursue them, will push us to the edges of how we have imagined not only justice but freedom."[4] As with other kinds of movements that promise redemption, asking for a more detailed program is often rebuked as a sign of insufficient faith: "Lack of imagination also indicates lack of commitment for figuring it out," writes Dunbar-Ortiz.[5]

In the meantime, there is critique. Because invasion is a structure, not an event, one way to combat it—perhaps the only way actually available today—is to deconstruct the social order founded by settler colonialism. This requires a double struggle: a public one against political and economic institutions, and a private one against the assumptions and behaviors that make us individually complicit, often in ways we hardly suspect until they are pointed out. These baleful legacies constitute "settler ways of being," a totalizing yet nonspecific term that makes it possible to blame virtually anything one objects to in modern American life—from selfishness to strip mining to the scientific method—on the original sin of settler colonialism.

At the level of theory, we have seen, the ideology of settler colonialism sets itself at odds with other social justice movements rooted in race, gender, or class. But in writing for a general audience about current political issues, practitioners of settler colonial studies usually converge on a familiar progressive agenda. Englert's denunciation of "capitalism, racism and dispossession," or Patel's of "the robbing of Black life at the hands of militarized law enforcement," could be cosigned by most liberals.

What's distinctive about settler colonialism as a tool of political analysis is that it sees all types of social injustice as flowing from a single source: the rapacity of European settlers. Historian Gerald Horne writes that America was born in the seventeenth century as a "hydra-headed monster" of "white supremacy and capitalism,"[6] and other theorists add new "heads" as needed. One widely cited online resource explains that "settler colonialism includes interlocking forms of oppression, including racism, white supremacy, heteropatriarchy, and capitalism."[7]

Of course, since the United States would not exist if not for European settlement, neither would its sins—or its virtues, if one believes it has any. But the claim that settler colonialism is behind every variety of social injustice goes beyond that tautology. It implies that settlers think about the world in a way that necessarily produces evil, today no less than in the seventeenth century. The continued existence of injustices like racism and sexism is proof that settler ways of being persist in us, and we in them.

For the ideology of settler colonialism, the essence of this evil disposition is insatiability. Starting with Wolfe, who wrote of "the insatiable dynamic whereby settler colonialism always needs more land,"[8] theorists have dwelt on the refusal of European settlers to be satisfied until they had engrossed entire continents—an idea once glorified in American history as "manifest destiny." Dunbar-Ortiz writes that "the very existence of the country is a result of the looting of an entire continent and its resources."[9]

Veracini points out that European colonialism was driven by an "expectation that every corner of the globe would eventually become embedded in an expanding network of colonial ties," as Marx and Engels wrote in *The Communist Manifesto*: "the need of a constantly expanding market for its products chases the bourgeoisie over the entire surface of the globe. It must nestle everywhere, settle everywhere, establish connections everywhere."

On this view, capitalism and colonialism are both expressions of a more primary insatiability in the soul of the settler, and of the Western civilization that produced him. That civilization long considered it heroic to refuse to be satisfied with the way things are; without dissatisfaction, after all, there would be no progress. The classic nineteenth-century formulation of this ethos was Tennyson's poem "Ulysses," in which the aged captain complains, "How dull it is to pause, to make an end," and vows "to strive, to seek, to find, and not to yield."

The European explorers who discovered the New World were once considered heroes in this mold. Bancroft began his *History of the United States* with Christopher Columbus, whose character he saw as prefiguring the virtues of America itself: he is the "daring navigator" who deserves "undivided glory" for his "immovable resoluteness" and the "grandeur of his conceptions."

Today's theorists of settler colonialism agree that America inherited the qualities of its first discoverer, but they have other qualities in mind. They dwell not on the

courage and skill that enabled Columbus to reach His-
paniola, but on what he did once he got there: abducting
dozens of the island's native Taíno people, seizing their
gold, forcing them into slavery, and killing anyone who
resisted. Columbus's actions, combined with the unwit-
ting introduction of European diseases, caused the population of the island to plummet by as much as 90 percent in
twenty years. And these evils have come to dominate our
imagination of Columbus. The History Channel, hardly
a hotbed of radicalism, marked Columbus Day 2019 with
an article on its website about the explorer's "extreme violence and brutality."[10]

For the ideology of settler colonialism, the insatiable demand for more—more power, more land, more
resources, even more knowledge—is not heroism but
rapacity, as when Horne refers to "rapacious colonialism"
or Englert to "rapacious . . . settler hunger." This rapacity is the nexus between colonialism and the "interlocking forms of oppression" it sponsors. In taking for granted
that he should grab as much of the world as he can, the
settler assumes that no one else has rights that need to
be respected.

A formal expression of this entitlement is the doctrine of
terra nullius, a concept in international law that designates a
certain territory as "land belonging to no one" and there-
fore free for anyone to take. Wolfe wrote that "Aborigines
were accorded no rights to their territory, informal vari-
ants on the theme of *terra nullius* being taken for granted

in settler culture." The earliest official formulation of this idea in Australian history is often located in an 1835 proclamation by Richard Bourke, the British governor of New South Wales, that canceled all land sales by Aborigines to colonists, on the grounds that Aborigines had no legal title in their land. Rather, the entire territory of the colony had the status of "vacant lands of the Crown" and could be occupied only by permission of the government.

This legal principle was not applied in North America, where settlers consistently acquired land from Native peoples by purchase and treaty. Though such transactions were often made under duress and on unfair terms, American law accepted the idea that Natives owned their land and had the right to dispose of it. Still, settler colonial studies often uses the term *terra nullius* in the American context, too, not in the strict legal sense but as a way of evoking settlers' arrogant entitlement. Dunbar-Ortiz writs that the idea of manifest destiny carried an "implication that the continent had previously been terra nullius, a land without people."[11] She finds the same implication in Woody Guthrie's song "This Land Is Your Land," whose praise of sharing the land is predicated on the assumption that it was free to be shared out in the first place.[12]

It is clear that what the ideology of settler colonialism censures as American insatiability and what patriotic historiography praised as American enterprise are one and the same quality. And perhaps both ways of evaluating that quality were equally useful in their time. In the early republic, when Americans faced the daunting task of conquering a continent, they looked to their past for examples of ambition and daring. Today, when Americans are striving to redefine their identity in multicultural terms and reduce their consumption of natural resources, they are looking to their past for lessons about the evils of greed and ethnocentrism.

Attributing those evils to an abstraction called settler colonialism, however, creates a serious obstacle to effective political action. It suggests that every desirable social outcome—economic equality, environmental conservation, sexual liberation, an end to racism—is not only compatible but in a sense identical. If settler colonialism is a hydra—or, as a group of public health experts wrote in 2023, "a shapeshifter with tools and technologies that evolve in conjunction with other oppressive structures (e.g., heteropatriarchy and white supremacy)"[13]—then once the monster is slain, all these evils will disappear at the same time. The great appeal of radical ideologies has always been this promise of a final solution. But history shows that once it becomes clear that slaying the hydra has not solved all problems—that different goals appeal to different constituencies and often require incompatible policies—the only solution radicalism can offer is to keep looking for shapeshifters, this time in its own ranks.

The ideology of settler colonialism offers a presentiment of this failure in its inability to specify what decolonization would actually mean or look like. It is a truism of settler colonial studies, for example, that the insatiability of colonialism is responsible for today's environmental crises. During Climate Week 2022, Columbia University's Climate School published an article on "How Colonialism Spawned and Continues to Exacerbate the Climate Crisis,"[14] explaining that some scholars reject the term *Anthropocene* because it "assumes the climate crisis is caused by universal human nature, rather than the actions of a minority of colonialists, capitalists, and patriarchs."

One of those scholars, Hadeel Assali of the Center for Science and Society, explained that "Western colonial legacies operate within a paradigm that assumes they can extract its natural resources as much as they want," while indigenous societies treat "the Earth as a precious entity that gives us life." It follows that the solution to the climate crisis—as to every other crisis—is decolonization. Only once this is achieved, Assali concluded, can we "finally start to envision a future that is different from the exploitative structures and institutions that we are now stuck within."

As always, the time to imagine what comes after settler colonialism is not yet. That may be because it is difficult to "envision a future" in which billions of human beings decide that they do not want things like cars, electricity, and cheap consumer goods, which can be produced only by extracting natural resources. The idea that settler colonialism is responsible for this insatiable appetite ignores the fact that, of the five countries with the highest carbon emissions in 2020, only the United States can be considered a settler colonial society. For China and India, the huge growth of their carbon emissions is in fact an anti-colonial victory, showing that countries formerly dominated by the West can achieve industrial might. Vietnam, which liberated itself from both French and American control, and as a Communist country is free even from the hydra-head of capitalism, saw its emissions of CO_2 triple between 2010 and 2020.

It is hard to see how decolonization, however defined, will reverse this state of affairs. Continued scientific progress might, but for the ideology of settler colonialism, science often appears as simply another expression of settler insatiability. This is partly because, as anthropologist Jennifer Raff writes in her book *Origin*, "Indigenous people have been treated with disrespect, condescension, and outright brutality by a number of scientists,"[15] with research agendas running roughshod over Native concerns about human remains and sacred sites. Raff tells the story of Kennewick Man, a nine-thousand-year-old skeleton discovered in Washington State in 1996, which became the subject of a legal dispute between scientists who wanted to study a unique specimen and Native American tribes who wanted to bury a distant ancestor. When the skeleton was interred in 2017, Raff writes, researchers saw it as "an incalculable loss of an important source of evidence about the past."

In other cases, she shows, researchers have earned the trust of Native peoples through open collaboration, demonstrating that science and Native rights don't have to be in conflict. For the ideology of settler colonialism, however, criticism of scientists' methods often passes over into criticism of the scientific method itself. When scientific explanations of nature or history refute the accounts of indigenous myth, even scientists are often reluctant to say so explicitly, fearful of repeating old offenses.

"I am a scientist," Raff declares, "and this book is about the past from a scientific perspective." Seen from that perspective, DNA and paleontological evidence make it clear that the earliest human beings to inhabit the Americas came from East Asia, perhaps as long as 25,000 years ago. Raff acknowledges that this account "conflicts with the understanding of some (though certainly not all) tribes of their own origins. They know that they have always existed in their lands; they did not travel from somewhere else." Yet she declines to say that, in this case, science is correct and myth is not, writing only, "I acknowledge this conflict but will not attempt to resolve it (if it is possible—or necessary—to resolve it at all)." The very use of the word *know* to describe mythical teachings, rather than *think* or *believe*, implies that science and myth are equally valid.

It is impossible to imagine people who call themselves progressive saying the same thing about, say, Christian beliefs. Indeed, the emancipation of reason from Christian doctrine was once the very definition of progress. For generations, European scientists struggled for the right to reject the biblical account of the age of the Earth and the origin of species. For Immanuel Kant, the motto of the Enlightenment was *Sapere aude*, "Dare to know."

But for settler colonial studies, this modern voracity for knowledge bears an uncomfortable resemblance to colonialism's insatiable desire for land. It's no coincidence that Wolfe's seminal book on settler colonialism was a critique of scientific anthropology, in which he named Kant as a source of the discipline's Eurocentrism. If the evil of colonialism has to do not merely with actions but with "ways of being," then science is at least as much to blame as capitalism or patriarchy.

To see what this means in practice, consider the Thirty Meter Telescope (TMT), an observatory planned for construction on Mauna Kea, an inactive Hawaiian volcano. The project has been in limbo since 2014, when some Hawaiians objected to the site on spiritual and environmental grounds. In a 2021 paper, Katherine G. Sammler and Casey R. Lynch, both professors of geography, don't simply endorse these concerns. They argue that the TMT is an example of how "Western scientific 'objectivity,'" along with categories such as "space, time, and matter," are themselves artifacts of settler colonialism.[16]

The problem isn't just that building an observatory on Mauna Kea might disregard the wishes of Native Hawaiians. Rather, by "collecting photons from the cosmic beginning, 13 billion years ago," the telescope "constructs a linear time progression backward toward the origins of the universe while evacuating the specificity of existing spatial relations on the island mountain." The implication is that time and space are not descriptions of reality but political constructs, imposed on indigenous peoples as a demonstration of power. This may sound outlandish, but it is simply an extension into the domain of physics of a principle commonly accepted when applied to ecology: that indigenous ways of being are essentially different from, and superior to, settler ways of being.

Political science is open to the same kinds of objections as physical science. In his book *Decolonizing Politics*, Robbie Shilliam of Johns Hopkins University complains that the discipline operates according to a "colonial logic" of "dividing humanity into oppositional categories with fixed properties," refusing "any consideration of peoples and places as flowing, shifting, and changing entities with relationships that increase and decrease in intensity."[17] Shilliam argues that "fixing reality in this extreme way must require—or at least, must lead to—violence." There is a direct path from "conceptualizing, diagnosing, and prognosing" to "apartheid," since both involve imposing boundaries: "Build a wall around a state. Build a wall around a neighborhood. Build a wall around your heart."

Arguments like these adapt some of the central tenets of deconstruction, the radical worldview of an earlier academic generation. For the French theorist Jacques Derrida, the original sin of Western thought was "logocentrism," a way of thinking that sees reason and language as capable of grasping ultimate reality. In his influential book *Of*

Grammatology, Derrida writes that the "logocentric longing par excellence is to distinguish one from the other," an arrogant ambition that he sees as quintessentially European: "Logocentrism is an ethnocentric metaphysicism, it is related to the history of the West."[18]

It is also quintessentially male, as he suggested in coining the term *phallogocentrism*, combining the Greek words for "reason" and "penis." Derrida's distrust of male, Western, scientific reason has been part of the climate of the academic humanities for decades. But where he imagined overcoming logocentrism by deconstructing it from within, settler colonial studies imagines repudiating it in favor of indigenous ways of knowing, which offer a "flowing, shifting" alternative to Western rigidity.

Thus it is not only political and economic institutions that cry out for decolonization. Abolishing settler colonialism means transforming the ways that we individually experience and understand the world. To avoid every practice that has been condemned as a settler way of being, one would have to renounce things like moving from one place to another ("As settlers create their claim on the land to which they have 'come to stay' precisely through technologies of mobility, they exert power and privilege by moving in and moving on just as much as through staying in and of itself")[19]; having a monogamous relationship ("Indigenous peoples . . . have been disciplined by the state according to a monogamist, heteronormative, marriage-focused, nuclear family ideal that is central to the colonial project.

Settler sexualities and their unsustainable kin forms do not only harm humans, but they harm the earth")[20]; and watching the Disney film *Moana* ("The ersatz Polynesian movie test-drove a twenty-first-century form of colonial-media expropriation of Native creative labor for collaborative, corporate storytelling").[21]

These statements were made in academic papers and lectures, which of course are not addressed to the general public. But ways of thinking that start out as academic and esoteric don't always stay that way. In fact, a generation educated in the ideology of settler colonialism has already begun to bring its principles into the public sphere. This has political consequences, as the pro-Hamas response to the October 7 attacks shows. But for many people, it also involves a more intimate process of repentance.

Here again, the analogy with Puritanism is striking. According to the logic of predestination, the first step toward being saved is accepting that one is damned, which leads to a certain paradoxical pride in acknowledging guilt. Just as born-again Christians declare that they are sinners, so practitioners of settler colonial studies often formally identify themselves as settlers. Tuck and Yang describe themselves as "an Indigenous scholar and a settler/trespasser/scholar writing together."

This practice is spreading outside the academy as well, especially in Canada. Shawn Cuthand, a Canadian Cree/Mohawk writer, observed in 2021 that it had become fashionable for "people [to] introduce themselves as 'settlers.'

Friends I have talked to refer to it as the fancy way of calling themselves white."[22] On X, a number of Canadian users now put "settler" in their bios. It is easy to imagine the practice becoming as standard etiquette in certain milieus, like stating one's preferred pronouns.

The collective equivalent of introducing oneself as a settler is the land acknowledgment. These are statements, read aloud on public occasions or displayed in permanent signage, in which an institution names the Native American peoples that once inhabited their site. For instance, Northwestern University's land acknowledgment states: "The Northwestern campus sits on the traditional homelands of the people of the Council of Three Fires, the Ojibwe, Potawatomi, and Odawa as well as the Menominee, Miami and Ho-Chunk nations." Even such a minimal statement is suggestive: Northwestern "sits" on other people's land, as if it might one day get up and walk away, leaving the land to its true owners. Similarly, the Seattle Art Museum "respectfully acknowledges that we are on Indigenous land, the traditional territories of the Coast Salish people": what is "on" can one day move "off," but the land will remain indigenous.

But land acknowledgments are usually more explicit and self-castigating. The Joyce Theater, a dance performance space in Manhattan, states that it "operates on the Lenape island of Manhahtaan (Mannahatta) and acknowledges that it was founded upon the stolen land and erasure of many Indigenous communities. This acknowledgement demonstrates our institution's commitment to the process of dismantling the legacies of colonialism and cultural imperialism." The Atlanta Contemporary Art Center says that it "occupies the land of the Mvskoke (Muscogee/Creek) Nation. These individuals were forcibly removed against their will and we reap the benefits of their turmoil. Our occupation of this land is an act of privilege."

Statements like these help to clarify what is really at stake in the discourse of decolonization. If the struggle against American settler colonialism were a real political struggle, like the ones waged against the French in Vietnam and Algeria, land acknowledgments would be contemptibly hypocritical, since the institutions that make them clearly have no intention of actually vacating the land they blame themselves for occupying. They are better understood as part of a rhetorical competition among "settlers" themselves, in which the confession of sin earns moral prestige.

For individuals who want to purge their sin by decolonizing themselves, there is a growing collection of texts and tools available. The website of the American Friends Service Committee, the venerable Quaker pacifist organization, offers a list of "Five Things You Can Do to Decolonize."[23] Tellingly, none of them are things you can actually do; rather, they are things you can say, secular equivalents to prayers, or what some Quaker congregations call "spiritual formation" exercises. Most of these are not even explicitly about decolonization, but general ethical affirmations such as "I am taking intentional time to be in an accountable honest relationship with others" and "I see the light in others and speak and act from that place."

These sentiments can be seen as decolonial only if one accepts the premise that spiritual states such as "emptiness," "loneliness" and "not-enoughness" are produced by settler colonialism, rather than being an inescapable part of human life, as religious traditions around the world have taught for millennia. "Colonialism has disconnected us from ourselves," this Quaker catechism teaches. But two thousand years ago, long before there were English settlers in America or even in England, the Apostle Paul described the same feeling in his epistle to the Romans: "For I do not do the good I want, but the evil I do not want is what I do" (Romans 7:19).

This book of the New Testament lay at the center of Martin Luther's theological revolution. Paul's description of the bondage of the will inspired the Protestant doctrine that human beings can be redeemed only by God's grace, not their own efforts. Perhaps this is why the ideology of settler colonialism arose in historically Protestant countries like Australia, Canada, and the United States: it offers a new, politically timely language for the traditional sense of being what Paul calls "a prisoner of the law of sin."

A religious language of sin and redemption can often be detected in settler colonial studies, even when writers themselves aren't fully conscious of it. In a 2017 essay on "Decolonizing Settler Colonialism," for instance, Veracini writes that the goal of his academic discipline is "to kill the settler in him and save the man."[24] He is alluding to an infamous speech by Richard Pratt, an American educator who declared in 1892 that the goal of schooling for Native American boys should be "to kill the Indian in him and save the man."

But both Veracini and Pratt are echoing the description of Jesus's sacrifice in the New Testament: "He himself bore our sins in his body on the cross, that we might die to sin and live to righteousness" (1 Peter 2:24). And for the ideology of settler colonialism, decolonization is often another name for dying to sin. This is clear in the many social media posts, blog entries, and student newspaper editorials in which self-identified settlers describe wrestling with their status.

Dying to sin is not the same thing as actually dying—in fact, it is the opposite—but Veracini takes pleasure in the violent sound of "kill the settler." "I recommend a Fanonian (and metaphorical) 'cull' of the settler," he writes, conscious that the two adjectives pull in opposite directions. Frantz Fanon, the most influential theoretician of decolonization in the 1950s, was part of the leadership of Algeria's FLN, who carried out their "culling" of French settlers with bombs and guns. In *The Wretched of the Earth*, Fanon wrote that for a liberation movement, killing settlers wasn't only a political tactic but a psychological necessity. In killing their oppressors, colonized people regain the humanity and confidence that have been taken from them: "The 'thing' colonized becomes a man through the very process of liberation." After a lifetime of being exploited, the colonized man finds dignified labor for the first time in killing: "To work means to work towards the death of the colonist."

Fanon's praise of violence is a large part of his appeal for Western intellectuals. Many of the sentiments expressed in *The Wretched of the Earth*, coming from a European or American writer, would immediately be identified as fascistic. There is Fanon's praise of militaristic nationalism, when "hearts begin to beat to the new national rhythm and they softly sing unending hymns to the glory of the fighters," or his lurid descriptions of killing: "Decolonization reeks of red-hot cannonballs and bloody knives." Under the banner of decolonization, fantasies of murder and hymns to national glory are rehabilitated for use by progressives.

In the introduction he wrote for Fanon's book, the French philosopher Jean-Paul Sartre suggested that this anti-colonial violence needs to be directed not only by Algerians against the French, but by the French against themselves: "We, too, peoples of Europe, we are being decolonized: meaning the colonist inside every one of us is surgically extracted in a bloody operation."

But there is a great difference between Fanon's bloody knives and Sartre's bloody scalpel. True decolonization movements, from the American Patriots of the 1770s to the FLN in the 1950s, used actual violence to drive out their oppressors. Intellectuals who use the language of settler colonialism to critique their own society, by contrast, have no mass movement at their back. That has been the predicament of the ideology of settler colonialism from the beginning: everyone knows that calls to "eradicate," "kill," or "cull" settlers can be only metaphorical, so there is no need to put a limit on their rhetorical ferocity.

But what if there were a country where settler colonialism could be challenged with more than words? Where all the evils attributed to it—from "emptiness" and "not-enoughness" to economic inequality, global warming, and genocide—could be given a human face? Best of all, what if that settler colonial society were small and endangered enough that destroying it seemed like a realistic possibility rather than a utopian dream? Such a country would be the perfect focus for all the moral passion and rhetorical violence that fuels the ideology of settler colonialism. It would be a country one could hate virtuously—especially if it were home to a people whom Western civilization has traditionally considered it virtuous to hate.

5

The Palestine Paradigm

In 2016 the Standing Rock Sioux, whose reservation spans the border of North and South Dakota and is home to about eight thousand people, launched a protest against the construction of the Dakota Access Pipeline, which was planned to carry oil underneath their land. Concerned that the project would disturb sacred ground and contaminate the water supply, protesters blocked equipment from a construction site and were aggressively dispersed with attack dogs and water cannons. The confrontation attracted international attention. Like Occupy Wall Street five years earlier, Standing Rock became a focus for many strands of progressive activism, including environmentalism, anti-capitalism—and perhaps more surprisingly, Palestinian liberation.

Stopping an oil pipeline in North Dakota and ending

the existence of Israel as a Jewish state might seem like very different goals, but to many progressives, they were two battlefields in the same struggle—against settler colonialism. In 2016 activists Amin Husain and Nitasha Dhillon founded Decolonize This Place, a New York City collective that started out by organizing pro-Palestinian protests at art museums. They soon began to demonstrate in solidarity with Standing Rock, on the grounds that it was impossible to talk "about Palestine—which is about occupation and settler colonialism and not talk about what does it mean to be part of, and complicit in, the settler colonialism happening here in the United States," as Husein later told an interviewer.[1]

Palestinian groups made a similar connection, using language familiar from the discourse of settler colonialism. The Palestinian BDS National Committee, which advocates for "boycott, divestment, and sanctions" against Israel, declared that "as indigenous Palestinians, we pledge to stand in solidarity with indigenous peoples around the world, including in Turtle Island." The Palestinian Youth Movement sent a delegation to Standing Rock to "stand together with our Indigenous siblings in the fight against corporate greed and the settler colonial state."

Standing Rock was a peaceful protest against constructing civilian infrastructure, while Gaza is a long-standing military conflict that has cost thousands of lives. But for the ideology of settler colonialism, both are cases of an illegitimate government abusing its power over an indigenous people. As Canadian academic M. Muhannad Ayyash put it in 2020, "the settler-colonial state's distinguishing feature is that it does not come into being and cannot continue to exist without claiming sovereignty over land that is forcefully taken from its native inhabitants. In short, the settler colony can only claim its sovereignty through the eradication and erasure of native sovereignty."[2] And since both the United States and Israel came into being against the will of the prior inhabitants of their land, everything they do is unjust. The question of whether the Dakota Access Pipeline would harm the Sioux, or how Israel ought to respond to deadly attacks from Gaza, are in a sense irrelevant, because they are merely practical. The more fundamental issue is that the United States and Israel do not have a right to govern at all.

Standing Rock was a key moment in what Australian theorist Rachel Busbridge called, in a 2018 paper, "the current groundswell in the application of the settler colonial paradigm to the conflict in Israel-Palestine."[3] Indeed, while the concept of settler colonialism was first developed to explain the history of Australia, Canada, and the United States, today it is perhaps most often invoked in connection with Israel. Settler colonial studies reflexively pairs Israel and the United States: Mamdani writes of "settler-colonial nation-state projects such as the US and Israel," while Veracini writes that "settler colonialism remains currently most invisible where a settler colonial order is most unreconstructed (e.g., Israel and the US)." In *The*

Routledge Handbook to the History of Settler Colonialism, Israel is the subject of three separate chapters (one on the biblical kingdom, two on the modern state), more than any country except the United States, which gets four.

Many Palestinian writers and activists have adopted the same terminology. In his 2020 book *The Hundred Years' War on Palestine*, Rashid Khalidi, a historian at Columbia University, calls Zionism a "classic nineteenth-century European colonial venture in a non-European land," whose goal was to create a "white European settler colony."[4] For Joseph Massad, Israel is a product of "European Jewish settler colonialism," and the "liberation" referred to in the name of the Palestine Liberation Organization is "liberation from settler colonialism."[5]

The insistence that Israel is the result of the same kind of settlement that created the United States, Canada, and Australia is puzzling on its face. As we have seen, settler colonialism is characterized by European settlers discovering a land that they consider *terra nullius*; their insatiable hunger for expansion that fills an entire continent; and the destruction of indigenous peoples and cultures. But the history of Israel does not include any of these hallmarks.

When modern Zionist settlement in what is now Israel began in the 1880s, Palestine was a province of the Ottoman Empire, and after World War I it was ruled by the British under a mandate from the League of Nations. Far from being "no one's land," Jews could settle there only by permission of an imperial government, and when that permission was withdrawn—as it fatefully was in 1939, when the British sharply limited Jewish immigration on the eve of the Holocaust—they had no recourse. Far from expanding to fill a continent, as in North America and Australia, the State of Israel today is about the size of New Jersey. The language, culture, and religion of the Arab peoples remain overwhelmingly dominant in the region: seventy-five years after Israel was founded, it is still the only Jewish country in the Middle East among twenty-two Arab countries, from Morocco to Iraq.

Most important, the Jewish state did not erase or replace the people already living in Palestine, though it did displace them. Here the comparison between European settlement in North America and Jewish settlement in Israel is especially inapt. In the seventy-five years after the first Puritan settlers arrived in Massachusetts, it is estimated that the Native American population of New England declined from about 140,000 to 10,000.[6] In the same number of years after 1948, the Arab population of historic Palestine more than quintupled, from about 1.3 million to about 7.5 million.[7] The persistence of the conflict in Israel-Palestine is due precisely to the coexistence of two peoples in the same land—as opposed to the classic sites of settler colonialism, where conflict between European settlers and native peoples ended with the destruction of the latter.

In the twenty-first century, the clearest examples of ongoing settler colonialism can probably be found in China.

In 2023 the UN Human Rights Council reported that the Chinese government had compelled nearly one million Tibetan children to attend residential schools "aimed at assimilating Tibetan people culturally, religiously and linguistically."[8] Forcing the next generation of Tibetans to speak Mandarin is part of a long-term effort to Sinicize the region, which also includes encouraging Han Chinese to settle there and prohibiting public displays of traditional Buddhist faith.

China has mounted a similar campaign against the Uighur people in the northwestern province of Xinjiang. Since 2017 more than a million Muslim Uighurs have been detained in what the Chinese government calls vocational training centers, which other countries describe as detention or reeducation camps. The government is also seeking to bring down Uighur birth rates through mass sterilization and involuntary birth control.[9]

These campaigns include every element of settler colonialism as defined by theorists like Wolfe and Veracini. They aim to replace an existing people and culture with a new one imported from the imperial metropole, using techniques described as genocidal in the context of North American history. Tibet's residential schools serve the same purpose as the ones established in Canada and the United States to "kill the Indian and save the man." And some scholars of settler colonialism have drawn these parallels, acknowledging, in the words of anthropologist Carole McGranahan, "that an imperial formation is as likely to be

Chinese, communist, and of the twentieth or twenty-first centuries as it is to be English, capitalist, and of the eighteenth or nineteenth centuries."[10]

Yet Tibet and Xinjiang—like India's rule in Kashmir, or the Indonesian occupation of East Timor from 1975 to 1999—occupy a tiny fraction of the space devoted to Israel-Palestine on the mental map of settler colonial studies. Some of the reasons for this are practical. The academic discipline mainly flourishes in English-speaking countries, and its practitioners usually seem to be monolingual, making it necessary to focus on countries where sources are either written in English or easily available in translation. This rules out any place where a language barrier is heightened by strict government censorship, like China. Just as important, settler colonial theorists tend to come from the fields of anthropology and sociology rather than history, area studies, or international relations, where they would be exposed to a wider range of examples of past and present conflict.

But the focus on Israel-Palestine isn't only a product of the discipline's limitations. It is doctrinal. To a degree that outsiders may well find surprising, for the ideology of settler colonialism, Palestine is the reference point for every type of social wrong. Building an oil pipeline under a Sioux reservation is like Palestine because both "make visible the continuum of systems of subjugation and expropriation across liberal democracies and settler-colonial regimes."[11] When the city of Toronto evicted a homeless encampment from a park, it was like Palestine because both are examples of "ethnic cleansing" and "colonial 'domicide,'" making Indigenous people homeless on their homeland."[12] Mental health problems among Native Americans are best understood in terms of Palestine, because the "hyper-visible Palestine case . . . provides a unique temporal lens for understanding settler colonial health determinants more broadly."[13] Pollution, too, should be understood through a Palestinian lens, according to the UK organization Friends of the Earth, because Palestine demonstrates that "the world is an unequal place" where "marginalized and vulnerable people bear the brunt of injustice."[14]

The problem with such comparisons is not that Palestinians in the West Bank and Gaza are not marginalized and oppressed. It is the notion that the only way to think about injustice, or even about basic historical phenomena like war and conquest, is by analogy with Palestine. For instance, Rosaura Sánchez and Beatrice Pita of UC San Diego write that "for Mexicans in the US Southwest, Nakba came in 1848."[15] Nakba is the Arabic name for the "catastrophe" of 1948, in which 750,000 Palestinians fled or were driven from their homes during Israel's war of independence. For Sánchez and Pita, this war, in which Israel conquered about 2,500 square miles of land that the UN had originally assigned to a prospective Palestinian state, is a paradigm for understanding the Mexican-American War, which took place one hundred years earlier and ended with Mexico ceding 525,000 square miles of territory to the United States.

Amir Husein describes the strategy of linking Palestine and Standing Rock as "collapsing a lot of concerns and problems together." This is intended as a positive description, and politically it has indeed been successful. As Busbridge writes, reconceiving the Palestinian cause as part of a global struggle against settler colonialism has contributed to "the slow but steady overturning of the default sympathy traditionally granted to Israel in favor of an increasing identification with the Palestinians."

In the American context, as we have seen, settler colonialism functions as an all-purpose explanation for capitalism, sexism, and climate change. Adding the Israeli-Palestinian conflict to the mix is powerfully energizing, giving a local address to a struggle that can otherwise feel all too abstract. The price of collapsing together such different causes, however, is that it inhibits understanding of each individual cause. Any conflict that fails to fit the settler colonial model must be made to fit.

This Procrustean process is never more conspicuous than when Western progressives insist that the struggle for LGBTQ rights and the struggle to liberate Palestine are one and the same. After October 7, a number of LGBTQ organizations in the United States declared their solidarity with Palestinians or even support for the Hamas attacks. Some of these groups, like Queers Undermining Israeli Terrorism (QUIT), were specifically devoted to Palestine activism, but others were simply LGBTQ advocates—like the New York City chapter of ACT UP, which announced in January 2024 that "we stand with Palestinians against a settler-colonial state backed by the finances and brutality of the U.S." The statement went on to compare Palestinians suffering under Israeli invasion in Gaza with the HIV patients the organization was founded to help in the 1980s.

The obvious problem with this stance is that Israel is far more supportive of gay rights than any other society in the Middle East. Tel Aviv has been called one of the most gay-friendly cities in the world, and Israel was one of the first countries to offer legal recognition of same-sex relation-ships. In Palestinian society, by contrast, homosexuality is strongly taboo and gay people are vulnerable to persecu-tion and violence—as became clear when Abu Murkhi-yeh, a twenty-five-year-old gay man, was murdered in Hebron in 2022 and a video of his beheading was posted on social media.

For Hamas, an Islamic fundamentalist organization, tol-erance of homosexuality is a primary example of West-ern sin and decadence. In a 2010 interview, Mahmoud Al-Zahar, a Hamas leader and onetime foreign minis-ter of the Palestinian Authority, told a European inter-viewer: "You do not live like human beings. You do not (even) live like animals. You accept homosexuality. And now you criticize us?"[16] Antigay and anti-Jewish hatred are complementary parts of the Islamist worldview, since both gays and Jews are beneficiaries of Western secularism, which Hamas seeks to destroy.

Yet the ideology of settler colonialism cannot make sense of this fact, because it is committed to the belief that all virtuous political struggles have the same enemy. For the American activist Sarah Schulman, boycotting Israel is a prerequisite of belonging to "the queer international, the global brotherhood and sisterhood of those who love justice," but criticizing Hamas is presumptuous: "Hamas was democratically elected. It doesn't matter what I think about Hamas."[17]

The Western left's sympathy with Third World anti-colonial movements has long been characterized by this kind of cognitive dissonance. The Tunisian Jewish writer Albert Memmi diagnosed it in his 1957 book *The Colonizer and the Colonized*, one of the classic texts of the decoloniza-tion era. "The leftist finds in the struggle of the colonized, which he supports a priori, neither the traditional means nor the final aims of that left wing to which he belongs," Memmi observed. "In fact, he is perhaps aiding the birth of a social order in which there is no room for a leftist as such, at least in the near future."[18] This was Memmi's own story: a supporter of Tunisia's struggle for independence from France, he left the country the same year his book was published, having found there was no place for a Jew-ish writer in a newly independent Arab country. Members of the "queer international" would find no warmer reception in Palestine.

To make Israel fit its ideologically allotted role, theorists of settler colonialism must similarly redefine two central concepts: indigeneity and genocide.

Contrary to many peoples' creation myths, no human population is literally indigenous, emerging primevally from their own land. Today's best genetic and paleontological evidence suggest that Homo sapiens originated in East Africa and gradually spread around the globe. When the term *indigenous* is used to describe Native Americans and Aboriginals, what it really refers to is priority: these peoples inhabited North America and Australia for a very long time, tens of thousands of years, before Europeans arrived.

In the discourse of settler colonialism, however, indigeneity has a meaning beyond chronology. It is a moral and spiritual status, associated with qualities such as authenticity, selflessness, and wisdom. These indigenous values stand as a reproof to settler ways of being, which are insatiably destructive. And the moral contrast between settler and indigene comes to overlap with other binaries—white and nonwhite, exploiter and exploited, victor and victim.

Until recently, Palestinian leaders preferred to avoid the language of indigeneity, seeing the implicit comparison between themselves and Native Americans as defeatist. In an interview near the end of his life, in 2004, PLO chairman Yasser Arafat declared, "We are not Red Indians." But today's activists are more eager to embrace the indigenous label and the moral valences that go with it. As the American academic Steven Salaita writes, "The term 'Indigenous' is infused with numerous connotations about access, belonging, biology, culture, jurisdiction, and identity. . . . To access that category is to be positioned as steward and legatee of a particular territory."[19] For Ahmad Amara and Yara Hawari of Al-Shabaka, a Palestinian think tank, the term "places indigenous knowledge and understanding, particularly resistance to invasion and attempts at erasure, at its core."[20]

In accordance with this idea, some theorists have begun to recast Palestinian identity in ecological, spiritual, and aesthetic terms long associated with Native American identity. Salaita has written that "Palestinian claims to life" are based in having "a culture indivisible from their surroundings, a language of freedom concordant to the beauty of the land."[21] Jamal Nabulsi of the University of Queensland writes that "Palestinian Indigenous sovereignty is in and of the land. It is grounded in an embodied connection to Palestine and articulated in Palestinian ways of being, knowing, and resisting on and for this land."[22]

This kind of language points to an aspect of the concept of indigeneity that is often tacitly overlooked in the Native American context: its irrationalism. Here is another instance where the ideology of settler colonialism takes a progressive route to a reactionary conclusion. The idea that different peoples have incommensurable ways of being and knowing, rooted in their relationship to a particular landscape, comes out of German Romantic nationalism. Originating in the early nineteenth century in the work of philosophers like Fichte and Herder, it eventually degenerated into the blood-and-soil nationalism of Nazi ideologues like Richard Walther Darré, who in 1930 hymned what might be called an embodied connection to Germany: "The German soul, with all its warmness, is rooted in its native landscape and has, in a sense, always grown out of it. . . . Whoever takes the natural landscape away from the German soul, kills it."[23]

For Darré, this rootedness in the land meant that Germans could never thrive in cities, among the "rootless ways of thinking of the urbanite." The rootless urbanite par excellence, for Nazi ideology, was of course the Jew. For Salaita, the exaltation of Palestinian indigeneity leads to the very same conclusion about "Zionists," who usurp the land but can never be vitally rooted in it: "In their ruthless schema, land is neither pleasure nor sustenance. It is a commodity . . . Having been anointed Jewish, the land ceases to be dynamic. It is an ideological fabrication with fixed characteristics."[24]

The greatest irony, however, is that in insisting that Palestinians are the indigenous people of Palestine, the ideology of settler colonialism finds itself unable to reckon with the Zionist principle that Jews are the indigenous people of the land of Israel. As Busbridge observes, "Rightfully or not, the notion of Jewish return inherent to Zionism means that Israel could be nothing if not 'native,'" and

THE PALESTINE PARADIGM
91

Zionism "could not have claimed so much success without the pervasiveness of the narrative that 'we were here first.'" But because recognizing Jews as aboriginal to the land of Israel would turn one of settler colonial studies' key rhetorical weapons against itself, it simply declines to engage with this idea and its implications.

Thus Sánchez and Pita declare that "the Palestinians are, in fact, the indigenous population of Palestine, which includes the territory now called Israel," just a few sentences after stating that "an indigenous population is one that has resided in an area for hundreds if not thousands of years and for whom that territory or soil is constitutive and defining of who the people are"—a formula that applies perfectly to Jews and the land of Israel. In his introduction to *The Routledge Handbook to the History of Settler Colonialism*, Veracini writes that chapters on "ancient and contemporary 'Israel'" are placed in different sections of the book in order to "emphasize discontinuity," because "insisting on continuity would reproduce a crucial tenet of Zionist ideology." Whether that tenet is true or not needn't be considered. Similarly, Khalidi complains that the Israeli-Palestinian conflict is not widely acknowledged as colonial because "Zionism . . . casts the new arrivals as indigenous and as the historic proprietors of the land they colonized," calling this an "epic myth," even though it is historically true.

In fact, if settler colonial studies weren't determined on ideological grounds to reject any Jewish connection to the land of Israel, it might find in Zionism an archetype of the kind of decolonization it hopes for in America. Here, after all, is a people that defined itself for centuries by its connection with the land where it came into being. It was driven out of that land by a mighty and ruthless empire, the Romans, who in the first and second centuries A.D. killed millions of Jews and drove millions more into exile. For a hundred generations, this people continued to pray every day for restoration to their homeland. Zionism translated this ancient spiritual aspiration into modern political terms and finally succeeded in restoring a remnant of the Jewish people to their aboriginal territory, just as another empire was killing millions of Jews in Europe.

If the dreamed-of decolonization of North America were to take place, wouldn't it resemble this story of exile and return? Even the language that the ideology of settler colonialism uses to refer to decolonization—"the memory/ dreams/fantasy of life before and beyond invasion," "maintaining memories of the worlds that were, as well as the worlds that can be"—echoes the language of Zionism. The Israeli national anthem, *Hatikva* (The Hope), declares that "the two-thousand-year-old hope will not be lost: / To be a free people in our land, / The land of Zion and Jerusalem." An early Zionist slogan was "If you will it, it is no dream."

In rejecting the idea that Jews are indigenous to the land of Israel, the ideology of settler colonialism aims to erase one of the central arguments for Zionism. The same goal lies behind its redefinition of genocide in such a way that the Jews, the exemplary modern victims of that crime, are transformed into its perpetrators instead.

Since the concept of settler colonialism was first elaborated by Patrick Wolfe, it has been defined by the destruction and replacement of an indigenous population. Wolfe argued that Israel is similar to Australia and the United States in this regard, comparing Israel's "continuing tendency to Palestinian expulsion" to Indian removal in nineteenth-century America, and warning in 2006 that the Jewish state was on the brink of committing a new Holocaust: "as Palestinians become more and more dispensable, Gaza and the West Bank become less and less like Bantustans and more and more like reservations (or, for that matter, like the Warsaw Ghetto)."[25]

Yet the facts stubbornly defy these comparisons. European settlement in Australia and America led to the destruction of existing populations, but Jewish settlement in Israel did not. Wolfe's reference to a "continuing tendency to Palestinian expulsion" appears to have been carefully worded to elide the fact that there was no continuing reality of Palestinian expulsion. The statement that Israel was concentrating Palestinians in a "Warsaw Ghetto" strongly implies that it was on the brink of exterminating them— that was the function of the actual Warsaw Ghetto, where Jews were concentrated before the Holocaust. But when Wolfe was writing in 2006, the Arab population of the West Bank and Gaza was approximately 3.6 million, and in 2023 it was 5.4 million—a stark contrast to the demographic trajectory of Jews in World War II Poland.

But if Israel is a settler colonial state, and settler colonialism entails genocide, then it is ideologically necessary for Israel to be committing genocide. This syllogism is largely responsible for settler colonial studies' ongoing effort to define genocide down, so that it no longer means what it is ordinarily taken to mean. When Wolfe wrote that settler colonialism is based on "the elimination of the native," the stark-sounding phrase turns out to have an equivocal meaning: it can refer to the physical elimination of a native people by killing, but also to any action inimical to "the native" as a distinctive way of life. In this sense, even policies that aim at equality between settler and native can be responsible for what Wolfe calls "structural genocide." For him, "romantic stereotyping" about indigenous life, "officially encouraged miscegenation," and "native citizenship" in the settler colonial state are all part of the "logic of elimination," no less than "frontier homicide" and "child abduction."

Veracini, as we have seen, attenuates genocide still further by defining it as any attempt to "transfer" a population from its native place, physically, socially, or even imaginatively. This allows him to place mass murder, cultural assimilation, and dressing up in native costume on the same spectrum, as expressions of "the transferist imagination." Veracini's choice of the word *transfer* is pointed, since it is commonly used in the context of Israel-Palestine to refer to the hypothetical future expulsion of Arabs to neighbor-ing countries. "Following and expanding on Palestinian scholar Nur Mashala's intuition that (Palestinian) 'transfer' is the foundational category in Zionist thought," Veracini writes, "all settler projects are foundationally premised on fantasies of ultimately 'cleansing' the settler body politic of its (indigenous and exogenous) alterities."

In this way, genocide, a crime actually committed against Jews in Europe, becomes merely a subcategory of transfer, a crime allegedly being planned by Jews in Israel. Veracini's terminology thus manages to imply that Jews bear at least as much responsibility for genocide as the Nazis who killed them. But then, equating Zionism with Nazism is commonplace in settler colonial studies. For Wolfe, set-tler colonialism of the type practiced in Australia and Israel is even worse than Nazism, because "in contrast to the Holocaust . . . settler colonialism is relatively impervious to regime change." Mamdani considers Israel the comple-tion of the Nazi project, since it "gave the Nazis what they had wanted all along: national homogeneity, by means of the ejection of Jews from Europe."

When Israel invaded Gaza after the October 7 attack, aiming to rescue hostages and destroy Hamas, it became commonplace on the left to accuse the country of com-mitting genocide. South Africa even brought charges of genocide against Israel at the International Court of Jus-tice. The invasion has brought death and suffering to Pal-estinians on a massive scale; yet it is notable that conflicts with far higher death tolls, some of them right next door in the Middle East, are never labeled genocides. Since 2011, up to 600,000 people have been killed in Syria's civil war, approximately ten times as many as have died in the entire Arab-Israeli conflict since 1948. Yet it took until 2023 for the country's dictator, Bashar al-Assad, to be charged at the International Court of Justice, and even then it was not with genocide but with violating treaties that ban torture.

The difference is that progressive discourse on Israel, shaped by the ideology of settler colonialism, defined the country as essentially genocidal long before 2023, creating a frame through which all of its actions are viewed. After all, if Israel is a settler colonial society, and settler colonialism is chiefly responsible for the world's material and spiritual suffering, then it is instinctively plausible for Israel, with its co-conspirator the United States, to be blamed for any kind of wrongdoing.

This idea can be seen at work in Steven Salaita's 2016 book *Inter/Nationalism: Decolonizing Native America and Palestine*. Salaita—who made headlines in 2014 when he lost a job offer from the University of Illinois for tweets such as "Zionists: transforming 'anti-Semitism' from something horrible into something honorable since 1948"—argues that "the relationship of Zionism with global systems of imperialism, militarization [and] plutocracy" makes Israel responsible for poverty and suffering around the world, as the linchpin of the "neoliberal" order that "pillage[s] resources and limit[s] economic development to the framework of profit-obsessed capitalism rather than allowing for the practice of legitimate egalitarian principles." The exact logic of the charge isn't clear, but the sentiment is. Salaita is restating, in the language of settler colonialism, ideas about Jewish greed and conspiratorial power that would have been perfectly at home in France during the Dreyfus Affair, or for that matter during the Middle Ages. So would his use of words like *perfidy* and *iniquity* to describe Israeli actions.

David Groulx, a Canadian poet with Ojibwe ancestry, expresses similar sentiments using different literary means. In his 2019 collection *From Turtle Island to Gaza*, he addresses a number of prominent Palestinian poets by name, seeing them as tribunes of an indigenous people, like himself. As a result, Israelis become a symbol of oppression in both Canada and Palestine. Groulx declares, "If Palestine was the size of Canada / they would have put you on reservations far off in the bush," evokes the monstrous figure of "a Settler's daughter" with "a star of David/in her mouth," and cries out, "Sing me Fanon / Sing me inferno."[26]

Such rhetoric makes it only too natural for young people educated in the ideology of settler colonialism to conclude that the conflict between Israel and the Palestinians embodies the conflict between good and evil in human history. Perhaps the most troubling reactions to the October 7 attacks were those of college students convinced that the liberation of Palestine is the key to banishing injustice from the world. In November 2023, the student newspaper of Northwestern University published a letter signed by sixty-five student organizations—including the Rainbow Alliance, Ballet Folklórico, and All Paws In, which sends volunteers to animal shelters—defending the use of the slogan "From the River to the Sea, Palestine Will Be Free." This phrase looks forward to the disappearance of any form of Jewish state between the Mediterranean and the Jordan, but the student groups denied that this entails "murder and genocide." Rather, they wrote, "When we say from the river to the sea, Palestine will be free, we imagine a world free of Islamophobia, antisemitism, anti-Blackness, militarism, occupation and apartheid."

As a political program, this is nonsensical. How could dismantling Israel bring about the end of militarism in China, Russia, or Iran? How could it lead to the end of anti-Black racism in America, or anti-Muslim prejudice in India? But one might as well ask how decolonizing Turtle Island would make it unnecessary to burn fossil fuels. For the ideology of settler colonialism, actual political conflicts become symbolic battles between light and darkness, and anyone found on the wrong side is a fair target—whether it's patients at New York's Memorial Sloan Kettering Cancer Center, where in January 2024 thousands of protesters chanted "MSK shame on you, you support genocide too" because they objected to a donor's politics, or Israeli civilians on a kibbutz.

In this way, anti-Zionism converges with older patterns of anti-Semitic and anti-Jewish thinking. It is true, of course, that criticism of Israel is not inherently anti-Semitic. Virtually anything that an Israeli government does is likely to be harshly criticized by many Israeli Jews themselves. But it is also true that anti-Semitism is not simply a matter of personal prejudice against Jews, existing on an entirely different plane from politics. In fact, the term *anti-Semitism* was coined in Germany in the late nineteenth century because the old term *Jew-hatred* sounded too instinctive and brutal to describe what was, in fact, a political ideology—an account of the way the world works and how it should be changed.

Wilhelm Marr, the German writer who popularized the word, complained in his 1879 book *The Victory of Judaism over Germanism* that "the Jewish spirit and Jewish consciousness have overpowered the world." That spirit, for Marr, was materialism and selfishness, "profiteering and usury." Anti-Semitic political parties in Europe attacked "Semitism" in the same way that socialists attacked capitalism. The saying "Anti-Semitism is the socialism of fools," used by the German left at this time, recognized the structural similarity between these rival worldviews.

The identification of Jews with soulless materialism made sense to nineteenth-century Europeans because it translated one of the oldest doctrines of Christianity into the language of modern politics. The Apostle Paul, a Jew who became a follower of Jesus, explained the difference between his old faith and his new one by identifying Judaism with material things—the circumcision of the flesh, the letter of the law—and Christianity with spiritual things—the circumcision of the heart, a new law "written not with ink but with the Spirit of the living God, not on tablets of stone but on tablets of human hearts" (2 Corinthians 3:3).

Today this characterization of Jews as stubborn, heartless, and materialistic is seldom publicly expressed in the language of Christianity, as in the Middle Ages, or in the language of race, as in the late nineteenth century. But it is quite respectable to say exactly the same thing in the language of settler colonialism. As the historian David Nirenberg has written, "We live in an age in which millions of people are exposed daily to some variant of the argument that the challenges of the world they live in are best explained in terms of 'Israel,'"[27] except that today Israel refers not to the Jewish people but to the Jewish state.

Massad, for instance, writes that "Israel is hardly exceptional in the annals of white settler-colonies but is rather exemplary" in "stealing the land of natives" by means of "stratagems," as well as in "the sadistic pleasure the colonists experience when suppressing indigenous resistance with maximum violence."[28] The word *exemplary* is well chosen: when the ideology of settler colonialism thinks about political evil, Israel is the example that comes instinctively to hand, just as Jews were for anti-Semitism and Judaism was for Christianity. Young people today who celebrate the massacre of Israelis and harass their Jewish peers on college campuses are not ashamed of themselves for the same reason that earlier generations were not ashamed to persecute and kill Jews—because they have been taught that it is an expression of virtue.

Why Israel Can't Be Decolonized

The left has long understood the Palestinian struggle against Israel as an anti-colonial movement. But as the definition of settler colonialism has changed over the decades, so has the meaning of anti-colonialism.

In the 1960s, when the paradigm of anti-colonial struggle was the Algerian war of independence, Palestinian militants saw themselves fighting another such war, with the Israelis playing the role of *pieds noirs*. The Palestinian Liberation Organization, founded in 1964, took the key word in its name from the Front de libération nationale, which had won Algeria's independence two years earlier.

Casting Israel as a colonial power helped the Palestinians win the support of European and American progressives who had once been favorable to the Jewish state, seeing it as a socialist society in the making. This shift accelerated after the Six-Day War in June 1967, when Israel conquered the West Bank from Jordan and the Gaza Strip from Egypt, bringing their Arab populations under military occupation. The same month *Les temps modernes*, the influential French journal of ideas edited by Sartre, published a landmark essay titled "Israel: Un fait colonial" ("a colonial fact"), by Maxime Rodinson, a scholar of Islam and a Jew whose parents were killed in Auschwitz.

In the essay, later published in English as the book *Israel: A Colonial-Settler State?*, Rodinson traced the history of Zionism and concluded that "wanting to create a Jewish, or predominantly Jewish, state in an Arab Palestine in the twentieth century could not help but lead to a colonial-type situation."[1] After all, Israel was created by Europeans, with the initial encouragement of the British Empire, against the will of the Arabs in Palestine. Anyone who condemned the creation of colonial societies in Algeria or Rhodesia, Rodinson concluded, had to condemn the creation of Israel on the same grounds: "even the slightest consistency in reasoning would have to rule out two different standards of evaluating and judging."

After making this historical case, however, Rodinson ends on a perplexing note. If Israel is a colonial society, it would be logical to conclude that the left should hope and work for its destruction, just as it did in the case of French Algeria. Yet Rodinson writes contemptuously about "left-wing intellectuals" who "preach vengeance and murder from an ivory tower." "The Jews of Israel too are people like other people," he writes—sounding a lot like Albert Camus, whose defense of his fellow French Algerians against terrorist violence earned the utmost contempt from the Sartrean left. Rodinson even ends his essay by recommending that the Arabs "resign themselves to a disagreeable situation" and grant "forgiveness for the injuries inflicted," which is as far from the spirit of Fanon as it is possible to get.

In calling Israel a *fait colonial*, Rodinson implies that it is also a *fait accompli*: perhaps creating the Jewish state was unjust, but destroying it would be a still greater injustice. This conclusion can be explained only by Rodinson's awareness of a key fact that his historical account downplays. The FLN victory in Algeria's war of independence was achieved by driving a wedge between French Algerians and France, whose military power the colonists relied on to protect their privileges. When the war began, French politicians of all stripes, including the Communists, adamantly insisted that Algeria was a part of France and could never be given up, any more than Normandy or Provence.

But both French Algerians and the country's native Arabs and Berbers knew that this was a political fiction. If holding on to the colony became costly enough, France could cut it loose, and if the *pieds noirs* feared living under the Algerians they had oppressed, they could always flee back to the mother country. The French Algerians fought this outcome with every means at their disposal, but in the end that is exactly what happened. When Algeria became independent in 1962, about 800,000 French Algerians, 80 percent of the total, immediately left for France.

Israel, however, has no mother country obligated to defend it, or to accept millions of refugees if it falls. Rodinson wrote in 1967 that if the country was destroyed, its people would be "cast into the sea," using an idiom that is still common today. Then as now, it is a euphemism for the murder of Israel's Jewish population—not a "structural" or "cultural" genocide but an actual second Holocaust, perpetrated on the same people as the first one. The October 7 massacre was a foretaste of exactly what being "driven into the sea" would mean for Israel's Jews.

The absence of a mother country is just one way that the history of Israel fails to fit the usual models of colonialism and anti-colonialism. Modern Jewish settlement in what is now Israel began at the same time that European powers like Britain, France, and Germany began the "scramble for Africa." But where those empires divided up a continent into huge colonies in order to exploit their people and resources, Jews went to Palestine in small volunteer groups, aiming to create self-sufficient agricultural communities. The first of these settlements, Rishon LeZion (Hebrew for "first in Zion"), was founded in 1882 by ten emigrants from Ukraine. The same year one hundred Romanian Jews founded Zikhron Ya'akov on a small plot of land purchased from an Arab landowner.

These groups did not have the backing of any government but were self-supporting or relied on private philanthropy. They were not drawn to Palestine by its natural resources, the way the Belgians valued the Congo for its rubber or the British valued South Africa for its diamonds, because the land had no such resources. Nor did they aim to exploit the native population, which to Kenneth Good was the economic definition of settler colonialism. On the contrary, the Labor Zionists who came to Palestine before World War I were determined not to employ Arab workers. They believed that Jews needed to be regenerated by engaging in agricultural labor, instead of the commercial and mercantile trades they practiced in Eastern Europe.

Nor, finally, did Jews come to Palestine in search of a higher standard of living, like the Europeans who settled in North Africa. If a colony, as Memmi wrote, is a place where people go "because jobs are guaranteed, wages high, careers more rapid and business more profitable," then Jewish Palestine was the opposite of a colony, since moving there usually meant a harder, poorer life. From the 1880s to the present day, the main driver of large-scale Jewish emigration to Israel has not been economic ambition but political persecution. It is a country built by refugees—from tsarist oppression in the early twentieth century, Nazism in the 1930s, Arab nationalist regimes after 1948, and the former Soviet Union in the 1990s. The State of Israel was recognized by the United Nations in 1948 in large part because hundreds of thousands of Jews were languishing in displaced persons camps in Europe with nowhere to go. And the Holocaust vindicated the central Zionist principle that the Jewish people need a country where no one can shut the doors against them.

Seeing Israel as a colonial state requires ignoring all these differences from true colonialism, resulting in a distorted picture not just of the country's history but of its possible future. The decolonization movement of the postwar decades triumphed across Asia and Africa for the same reason that the American Revolution succeeded two centuries earlier: An empire's will to keep control of distant colonies is always weaker, in the long run, than the colony's will to self-determination. This is simply because the empire's soldiers and administrators have a home to go back to, while a colonized people have no other home but the one they're fighting for. The same logic explains why the long American interventions in Vietnam and Afghanistan ended in failure: all the Communists and the Taliban had to do was wait for the United States to get tired of losing lives and money.

If Israel is a colonizing power, then the struggle for Palestinian liberation should be able to succeed by using the same tactics as the Vietcong or the FLN—or for that matter, the Irgun, the Jewish terrorist group that helped drive the British out of Palestine after World War II. A campaign of attacks and atrocities against civilians would eventually sap the colonizer's will to resist. But the fact is that Israel's 7 million Jews have no other home to go to. They or their ancestors left their former countries after suffering persecution and genocide, never to return. That is why they will fight for their country, not like the French in Algeria or Vietnam, but like the Algerians and Vietnamese.

Israel's neighboring Arab states came to a tacit acceptance of this fact in the 1970s, putting an end to decades of attempts to invade the Jewish state and wipe it off the map. The Palestinians have not, which is a major reason why the Israeli–Palestinian conflict continues, seventy-five years after the foundation of Israel and almost 150 years after Zionist settlement began. But it makes sense that the Palestinians are unable to acknowledge that the Jews are in the situation of a native people rather than a colonizer, for in relation to the Arabs of Palestine, Israel does resemble a colonial power.

The chief resemblance is that Israel, like European colonies around the world, was created without the consent of the people already living there. For Khalidi, "the modern history of Palestine can best be understood . . . as a colonial war waged against the indigenous population, by a variety of parties, to force them to relinquish their homeland to another people against their will."

This was not how the first Zionists understood what they were doing. Until World War I, Jewish settlers generally told themselves that the creation of a prosperous Jewish society in Palestine would benefit the Arabs living there as well. Theodor Herzl, who convened the first World Zionist Congress in 1897, wrote a speculative novel called *Old New Land* in which the only Arab character, Reschid Bey, offers gratitude for Zionism: "The Jews have enriched us.

Why should we be angry with them? They dwell among us like brothers. Why should we not love them?"

But actual Palestinian Arabs did not share this complaisant attitude, and as the Jewish population grew—reaching some sixty thousand by 1914—Arab opposition became undeniable. A key turning point came in November 1917, when the British, then engaged in conquering Palestine from the Ottoman Empire, issued the Balfour Declaration, stating their support for "the establishment in Palestine of a national home for the Jewish people." The term *national home* didn't necessarily mean an independent Jewish state, but it didn't rule one out, either; and unlike the Turks, the British were open to large-scale Jewish immigration, at least initially.

For the first time, the Balfour Declaration made it conceivable that Palestine would become a Jewish country. This was a triumph for Zionism, but for the Arabs, Khalidi writes, "Balfour's careful, calibrated prose was in effect a gun pointed directly at their heads, a declaration of war by the British Empire on the indigenous population." Over the next twenty years, armed conflict between Jews and Arabs escalated, spurring the formation of a Jewish militia that would evolve into the Israeli Defense Forces.

In this transformed situation, Vladimir Jabotinsky, an aggressive Jewish nationalist, broke with mainstream Zionist organizations by insisting—or acknowledging—that the Arabs would never voluntarily accept a Jewish state in Palestine. In his 1923 essay "The Iron Wall," Jabotinsky wrote that "every native population, civilized or not, regards its lands as its national home, of which it is the sole master, and it wants to retain that mastery always; it will refuse to admit not only new masters but even new partners or collaborators. This is equally true of the Arabs."[2]

It followed that for Zionism to succeed in creating a Jewish homeland, it would need armed force, either Britain's or its own: "It can proceed and develop only under the protection of a power that is independent of the native population—behind an iron wall, which the native population cannot breach." One way or another, Israel has lived by this principle ever since. Today Jabotinsky's iron wall lives on in the Iron Dome, the antimissile system that Israel relies on to intercept rocket attacks.

As late as 1947, when Britain announced that it would withdraw from Palestine, Arabs outnumbered Jews by two to one. Yet two decades later Israel controlled the entire territory between the Jordan River and the Mediterranean Sea. This transformation took place in three steps. First, in 1947, the United Nations proposed to divide Palestine into two states, one for Jews and one for Arabs. The Jews accepted partition while the Arabs rejected it, in keeping with their consistent opposition to the creation of a Jewish state in their midst.

When Israel declared independence in May 1948, an already bloody guerrilla conflict turned into open warfare, as the new country fought against the armed forces of the Palestinian Arabs as well as five neighboring Arab states.

The Israelis won the war, largely due to superior organization; Khalidi writes that the Palestinians were "facing the well-developed para-state of the Jewish Agency without having a central state system themselves." In the course of the fighting, Israel annexed some of the land designated by the UN for a Palestinian state, while about 750,000 Arabs were driven out of or fled from Israeli territory in the Nakba. About 150,000 Arabs remained in the Jewish state, and today the Arab population of Israel numbers about 2 million.

No Palestinian state came into being on the remaining land because the West Bank and the Gaza Strip, with their new population of refugees, were annexed by Jordan and Egypt, respectively. That remained the case until 1967, when Israel, facing an imminent threat of invasion from Egypt, preemptively launched the Six-Day War. In a shockingly rapid campaign, Israel conquered the West Bank and Gaza, bringing the whole of historic Palestine under its control.

In 1967, unlike in 1948, Israel did not seek to annex the conquered territory or to expel its Arab inhabitants. But it also didn't withdraw and return the land to Egypt and Jordan, or allow the creation of an independent Palestinian state. Instead it held the West Bank and Gaza under military occupation, in which the Arab inhabitants had limited rights. More than fifty years later Israel remains in control of the West Bank, though much of it is now administered by the Palestinian Authority. In 2005 Israeli forces withdrew from Gaza; two years later Hamas came to power in the small, densely populated territory, and has used it as base for periodic attacks on Israel ever since.

Today the Jewish and Arab populations living between the Mediterranean Sea and the Jordan River number about 7 million each. This parity makes clear that the settler colonial model, based on one people eliminating and replacing another, does not describe the Israeli-Palestinian experience. Israel governs some 3 million Arabs in the West Bank, without their consent; another 2 million Arabs live under Hamas rule in Gaza; and 2 million Arabs are Israeli citizens, legally if not socially equal to Israeli Jews.

The complexity of this situation is the result of a great number of historic events occurring in a small territory in a short time. In Israel-Palestine, if anywhere, the Wolfean maxim "invasion is a structure not an event" is revealed to be much too limited. In fact, every national border, legal regime, and economic disparity everywhere in the world is the aftermath of an event, and not just one event but the whole accumulation of them that constitutes history. That is why arguments about the future are always implicitly arguments about the past. To judge the world we live in is to interpret how it got this way.

In the case of Israel-Palestine, the big question is when things began to go wrong. Was it in 1967, when Israel occupied the West Bank and Gaza, bringing millions of Arabs under its control? Many American and Israeli liberals think so, and believe that 1967 must be revoked by turning those territories into a Palestinian state. But the majority of Israelis disagree. After all, Israel occupied the territories in the first place because the country's internationally recognized border left it vulnerable to repeated invasions. In December 2023 a poll by the Palestinian Center for Policy and Survey Research, an independent nonprofit based in Ramallah, found that 72 percent of Palestinians approved of the October 7 attack on Israeli civilians.[3] Does this offer any encouragement for returning to what the Israeli diplomat Abba Eban long ago called "Auschwitz borders"?

For many Palestinians, on the other hand, undoing 1967 would not go far enough. The minimum acceptable solution would be to turn the clock back even further by undoing the Nakba, allowing the descendants of the refugees of 1948 to reclaim the land and homes their ancestors lost inside Israel. Palestinians themselves are divided about which of these goals should take priority. In a 2021 poll, 47 percent of Palestinians saw the creation of a Palestinian state in the West Bank as the most important goal, while 34 percent said it was most important for descendants of refugees to return to lands and homes lost in 1948.[4]

Since those descendants now number some 5 million, the result would be to erase Israel's Jewish majority and ultimately its character as a Jewish state and homeland. For Israelis, this is an existential red line that can never be crossed; in 2018 Prime Minister Benjamin Netanyahu said that "the so-called 'right of return'" for Palestinian refugees had "the aim of eliminating the State of Israel."[5]

This Israeli view implicitly acknowledges that the original expulsion of the refugees of 1948 was necessary for a Jewish state to exist at all.

The intractability of the conflict has vindicated Jabotinsky's view, regarded by mainstream Zionists at the time as brutally pessimistic, that the aims of Jews and Arabs in Palestine could not be peacefully reconciled. The moment the Zionist movement began to work for a Jewish homeland in Palestine, it set itself on a collision course with Arab desires and aspirations, and only force could determine who would prevail. Israel exists because so far, the Jews have prevailed at crucial moments. If it ceased to prevail even once, it would be destroyed.

This Zionist realism is fundamentally congruent with the Palestinian nationalist view, which sees the history of Israel as that of a foreign people inexorably taking over an Arab country. The difference is that for Zionists, the creation of a Jewish state was justified by historic claims and existential necessity. Without Israel, the Jewish people would have been even more thoroughly destroyed in the Holocaust than it was. Since 1948, meanwhile, Jews have flourished as never in the past two thousand years—not only in Israel but in the Diaspora as well.

For Palestinians, these are not good enough reasons to justify their loss and suffering. They believe the Zionist project was illegitimate from the start, which implies that history must be rolled back not to 1967 or 1947 but to

1880, before modern Jewish settlement began. The problem with rectifying history by deleting Israel, however, is what to do with the 7 million Jews who now live there. The humane answer is that they could continue to do so, just not in a Jewish country. Instead there would be a single state with roughly equal numbers of Jews and Arabs, at least to begin with. This solution has appealed to everyone from the liberal Jewish intellectual Tony Judt to Libya's dictator Muammar Gaddafi, who in 2000 called for the creation of a new country called Isratine.[6]

Khalidi is more ambiguous, advocating "complete equality of rights, including national rights," without specifying whether this would be implemented in one or two states. But whatever form it takes, he makes the crucial point that only a solution based on "mutual acceptance" between Jews and Arabs can be morally acceptable, since the only alternative is "the unthinkable notion of one people's extermination or expulsion by the other."

This is the crucial dividing line between solutions, and advocates for those solutions, that can be called liberal and humane, and those that are dangerous and cruel. The tragedy of Israel-Palestine is that it is harder to imagine the humane futures coming true than the cruel ones. It hardly seems possible that Jews and Arabs who are mortal enemies under different governments would become good neighbors living under the same government. Nor is it likely that Hamas, which as a paramilitary group devotes so much effort to killing Jews, would be less interested in killing Jews (or less effective at it) if it ran a full-fledged state and military.

On the other hand, it is all too easy to imagine the eventualities Khalidi calls "unthinkable." In Israel, religious and political extremists hope to repeat the Nakba by expelling Arabs from the occupied territories into Egypt or Jordan. Among the Palestinians, religious and political extremists hope to cleanse the Jews from what they see as Arab, Islamic land. Since Egypt and Jordan would assuredly not accept millions of Jewish refugees, this would mean driving them "into the sea," that is, killing them. On both sides, these elements seem to have more momentum and passion than those working for peaceful coexistence.

Western intellectuals seldom openly endorse the eliminationist ambitions of either Jews or Arabs, and the leading ideologues of settler colonialism do not call for Israelis to be pushed into the sea. Mamdani recommends "de-Zionization," a one-state solution that would make Israel "a state for all its citizens."[7] Veracini argues for a two-state solution, at least initially: "the Palestinian Authority (PA) and/or a Hamas-led government in Gaza could end up inheriting the occupation's structures and fashion their rule as postcolonial successor polities," though this would not liberate Arab Israelis, whom he calls "Palestinians who have been subjected to the successful settler colonial project that is Israel."[8]

But the actual effect of the ideology of settler colonialism is not to encourage any of these solutions. It is to cultivate hatred of those designated as settlers and to inspire hope for their disappearance. In this way, it abets Arab rejection of the State of Israel, which has helped to freeze the Israeli-Palestinian conflict in the same basic form since before 1948. The hope that Israel will prove to be a short-lived aberration, a historical curiosity like the Crusader kingdoms of the Middle Ages, condemns the Palestinians to political limbo, the Jews to aggressive hypervigilance, and both to dreams of a final solution in which the enemy simply disappears. Insofar as the ideology of settler colonialism nourishes such dreams, it helps to ensure a worse future for everyone living "between the river and the sea."

7

Justice and Despair

"For many who are tuned in to what Walter Benjamin called 'the tradition of the oppressed,'" writes John Collins of St. Lawrence University, "the centrality of Palestine is almost axiomatic."[1] But an axiom is not a truth; it is a statement that must be accepted as true in order for a system of thought to function. For the ideology of settler colonialism, Palestine is axiomatic in just this sense: it is a premise from which many conclusions are drawn, and not just about Israel. The fact that many of these conclusions are false and harmful should lead us to question whether the axiom is sound. Is there a better way to think about the tradition of the oppressed, and what can be done to redeem it?

Walter Benjamin, the German Jewish philosopher and critic, coined the phrase "the tradition of the oppressed" in his last major essay, "On the Concept of History," written in early 1940. At the time, he was living in Paris as a refugee from Nazism. A few months later Germany conquered France, forcing Jewish exiles like Benjamin to flee for their lives. In September he was one of a group of refugees who attempted to cross the border into Spain, hoping eventually to make it to the United States. But the party was intercepted by border guards, and Benjamin, in despair, killed himself with an overdose of morphine.

Despair in the face of historical evil is the subject of "On the Concept of History." In a series of short reflections, Benjamin argues that in the twentieth century it is no longer possible to believe in the idea of progress, which lay at the heart of nineteenth-century social thought. At a moment when Nazism appeared triumphant, Benjamin came to believe that the injustice and barbarity around him were humanity's essential condition. "The tradition of the oppressed teaches us that the 'state of emergency' in which we live is not the exception but the rule," he writes. Rather than trying to accelerate the course of history, then, our duty is to resist it—"to brush history against the grain."

In the twenty-first century, Benjamin's heretical way of thinking about history and progress has become the common conviction of many people in the West. When we look at the past, we see it through the eyes of the figure Benjamin called, in the same essay, "the angel of history," whose eyes are fixed on the past while a storm "irresistibly propels him into the future." "Where we perceive a chain of events," Benjamin writes, "he sees one single catastrophe which keeps piling wreckage and hurls it in front of his feet."

Just so, when we look at historical episodes that our ancestors saw as glorious and righteous, our eyes are drawn to the wreckage they neglected. Where they saw Christopher Columbus as a champion of progress, we see the people he killed, enslaved, and infected. Where they saw the American Revolution as a new birth of freedom for humanity, we see how George Washington and Thomas Jefferson were sustained by slavery. And where many Americans, not only Jews, once understood the founding of the State of Israel as the miraculous rebirth of a destroyed people, today many Americans, including many Jews, see it as a crime against the Palestinians.

The ideology of settler colonialism is founded on this shift in moral perspective. For liberals who acknowledge the moral claim of the tradition of the oppressed, this makes it difficult to criticize, just as with earlier ideologies of the left like Jacobinism or Communism. For many Jews, in particular, it is intolerable to feel that they have moved from the status of victim to that of victor, since they feel like Benjamin that it is a duty to "call in question every victory, past and present, of the rulers."

Yet Benjamin's essay is ambivalent about what, if anything, can be done to rectify the catastrophe of history. In some sections, he suggests that fascism can be stopped by a working-class revolution, and he blames the leaders of German socialism for misdirecting the movement. But in others, like the "angel of history" section, he seems to suggest that it would take a divine intervention to wrench history out of its evil course. In these moments Benjamin sounds less like a Marxist than a mystic awaiting the coming of the Messiah. For Judaism, he writes at the end of the essay, "every second of time was the strait gate through which Messiah might enter."[2]

In vacillating between extreme violence and extreme passivity—making the revolution or waiting for the Messiah—Benjamin testifies to the hopelessness of his historical moment. For him, as for tens of millions of others who were about to die in World War II, there was no possibility of being saved. The only way he could envision redemption was as the cancellation of history.

The ideology of settler colonialism is founded on a similar sense that history is evil and deserves to be repealed. When Dunbar-Ortiz says that the European discovery of America is something that "should not have happened," she is writing in a Benjaminian spirit. And this intuition contains an undeniable kernel of truth. If history is, as Edward Gibbon wrote in *The Decline and Fall of the Roman Empire*, "little more than a register of the crimes, follies and misfortunes of mankind," then anyone who manages to "make history" is a malefactor by definition. For Benjamin, this truth contaminates even the "cultural treasures" that seem like the most worthy and innocent products of the past. "There is no document of civilization which is not at the same time a document of barbarism," he writes in "On the

Concept of History." This applies to the Declaration of Independence no less than to the Pyramids, both pinnacles of civilization that could not have existed without slavery.

The ideology of settler colonialism feels this indignation against the past in its bones, and dreams of a future in which the past is rectified. This is understandable and even praiseworthy, especially for young people who are just becoming aware of history. But the call to decolonize Turtle Island and liberate Palestine "between the river and the sea" is based on the same kinds of moral and political error as earlier radical movements that appealed to idealists and intellectuals.

First, the ideology of settler colonialism turns its wrath not on the most deserving targets but on those that are closest to hand. Its adherents believe that the United States, Canada, Australia, and Israel have a uniquely vicious "way of being," responsible for a history of genocide, ecocide, sexism, racism, and insatiable greed. But what they have discovered is only the local manifestation of what Benjamin recognized as a universal truth: that history itself is a state of emergency. Only a few countries and eras are tainted by settler colonialism, but there is not a single country whose history does not provoke horror, if seen through the eyes of the victims rather than the victors.

For every atrocity that we twenty-first-century Americans are familiar with—the Holocaust, the African slave trade—there are a dozen more we forget or never knew. Mao Zedong was not a settler colonialist, but his regime was responsible for the deaths of 80 million Chinese. The Thirty Years' War was fought over religion and great-power politics, not colonial territory, but it killed 8 million people in seventeenth-century Germany, a third of the total population. Pre-Columbian America is no exception to this rule: the history of the Aztec and Inca empires is full of battles in which tens of thousands of soldiers were killed.

The mantra of settler colonial studies is that "invasion is a structure, not an event," but if this true in North America, it is equally true everywhere else. Why is Russia the largest country in the world by land area? Why does India have the world's third-largest Muslim population? Why is English spoken, not just in former parts of the British Empire, but in the British Isles themselves? The answer in every case is invasion and settlement—the replacement of one people and culture by another. As far back as we can see, there is no *terra nullius* and no true indigeneity. Every people that occupies a territory took it from another people, who took it from someone else.

This is just as true of Native Americans as of other peoples, except that the absence of written records makes the chain of conquest impossible to discern. Land acknowledgments often include a statement that a certain tribe has occupied a given territory from "time immemorial," but all this really means is that the people in question were there when Europeans or Americans arrived. How the land changed hands in the tens of thousands years prior is unknowable.

Until fairly recently, the idea that states originate in war and conquest was not a scandal but a truism. Giambattista Vico, the eighteenth-century Italian philosopher, wrote that "all commonwealths were brought into being by force of arms and then composed by laws."[3] And nations traditionally took pride in their martial origins. In the *Aeneid*, Virgil's patriotic epic about the beginnings of the Roman Empire, Jupiter prophesies that Aeneas "shall tame fierce nations in the bloody field, / And sovereign laws impose, and cities build."[4]

Of course, the fact that this idea was once common does not mean that it was right. Like slavery and the divine right of kings, the glory of conquest is one of those ancient truths that modern humanity now finds hateful and strives to overcome. In every such moral revolution, the desire to build a better future has a tendency to create a feeling that the past is contaminated and must be destroyed. When the Protestants of sixteenth-century Europe stripped the altars and artworks from their churches and painted them white, or when the French Revolutionaries instituted a new calendar starting with the year zero, they were expressing this kind of revulsion at the past. But the past can't be rectified so easily, because history cannot stop and restart. It just keeps going, and the revolution itself is remembered as just another bloody chapter.

For the ideology of settler colonialism, the impossibility of concretely imagining a decolonial future ought to serve as a warning sign. It is possible to look forward, in general terms, to a future in which the United States disappears and indigenous life continues. But it is hard to envision getting from here to there without destruction and suffering on such a vast scale that even the partisans of decolonization refuse to discuss it. Israel is much younger and smaller than the United States, and it is easier to imagine its disappearance, but again, not without massive death and destruction. When activists use the slogan "from the river to the sea, Palestine will be free," yet refuse to spell out exactly what this means and how it will be accomplished, they are blinding themselves to the reality of their own desires.

Decolonization was able to succeed in Africa and Asia because the European intervention into the histories of those places was violent but shallow. In redefining settler colonialism, theorists starting with Patrick Wolfe suggested that a similar remedy could be applied in places where settler society was massive and deeply rooted. But in North America and Australia, nonindigenous people do not understand themselves as settlers, because there is no native majority to contrast themselves with. On the contrary, they call themselves natives, or immigrants on the way to becoming natives.

This very innocence is what enrages the ideology of settler colonialism. Tuck and Yang denounce "settler moves to innocence," in which settlers acquit themselves of wrongdoing by sentimentalizing their relationship with natives or equivocating about their own role. But the real reason why settlers feel innocent is that, as Tuck and Yang complain, they have "an absence of experience of oppressive power." They do not feel that they have oppressed any native people, because they actually have not. And the reason they haven't is that their ancestors, or the ancestors of their fellow citizens, replaced the native population so effectively. Today's innocence is the product of yesterday's guilt; as Benjamin says, every document of civilization is a document of barbarism.

We can't revoke the past and its barbarisms, but it is very much in our power to express our hatred of the past by inflicting new barbarisms. In North America, calls for decolonization cannot restore lost languages and civilizations, or make hundreds of millions of "settlers" disappear, or uninvent the technology that made hunter-gatherer societies obsolete. But such calls can lead people to despise their country and see its institutions as worthy of destruction.

Meanwhile, in Israel, where the prospect of driving settlers "into the sea" appears very real, the language of settler colonialism falsifies history in order to dehumanize Israeli Jews and celebrate their deaths. The Hamas attacks of October 7 were a document of barbarism, if anything ever was; yet to the ideology of settler colonialism they were praiseworthy, because they were seen as an attempt to rectify historical injustice.

Perhaps the best way to describe the error of this way of thinking is that it embraces the wrong kind of despair. The suggestion that there can be a right kind of despair might seem bizarre, since we are used to thinking of hope as the most important political virtue, the thing that makes progress possible. But hope and despair go together in unexpected ways.

For Benjamin in 1940, the future offered only reasons for despair, so his hope had nowhere to lodge but in the past. "The past," he wrote, "carries with it a temporal index by which it is referred to redemption." The idea of redemption, which stands at the core of Benjamin's thought, is hope directed backward: all the suffering that brought us to this unbearable moment will be negated, liquidated. That is why redemption entails destruction, whether it takes the form of a political revolution or a messianic advent. "The Messiah comes not only as the redeemer, he comes as the subduer of Antichrist," Benjamin notes.

The ideology of settler colonialism shares this longing for redemptive destruction. Its eyes fixed on what it takes to be the worst parts of history, it insists that they deserve to be undone. But this idea can seem plausible only in moments of utter desperation. In reality, the past cannot be redeemed because history cannot be undone. Revolutionary movements become savage when they confront this truth, as sooner or later they must. So, too, with the ideology of settler colonialism: the impossibility of true decolonization impels the discourse about it to become more extreme, conspiratorial, and violent.

Despair of the future forces us to place our hope in remaking the past. But if what we want is hope for the future—for the possibility of ending conflicts, rather than renewing them; for reconciliation, rather than righteous hatred—then it may be necessary to despair of the past. This would mean recognizing that the wounds we inherit can't be undone, but perhaps they can be healed, even if they're guaranteed to leave a scar.

A model for this kind of despair can be found in the Talmud's discussion of the legal status of lost and stolen items. If a person loses a possession or has it stolen, does he remain its legal owner? It might seem obvious that he should: after all, he never agreed to give it up. But suppose a thief stole a cloak and sold it to a merchant, who sold it to a customer. If the garment still belongs to the original owner, then he would have the right to go to the customer and take it back. In remedying the original wrong, however, this would create a new wrong, since the new owner acted in good faith and paid for his purchase.

Now imagine a case involving not just a cloak but homes, land, and political sovereignty, over a span of centuries. Land acknowledgments suggest that the land on which an institution is built still belongs, in some sense, to the Native American tribe that once lived there. But if that tribe went to court to evict the university or museum making the acknowledgment, on the grounds that their ancestors never intended to relinquish ownership, the institution would surely counter that this claim could not be enforced—due to the passage of time, the unclear chain of title, and its own innocence. A legal system that held out hope of reversing every loss would create more chaos and injustice than it remedied.

For this reason, Jewish law introduces the concept of "despair."[5] Under certain circumstances, the law presumes that a person who loses a possession despairs of getting it back and thus relinquishes ownership. The Talmud's examples include coins lost in a public place, a donkey taken by a customs collector, and a garment stolen by a bandit. A person who despairs is still entitled to monetary compensation and damages, but he or she can no longer demand the return of the original item, and its subsequent chain of title is valid.

Is despair justice? No. It is what the law offers instead of justice, knowing that perfect justice often cannot be achieved. And what is true of individuals and their possessions is infinitely more so of nations and their histories. To render perfect justice, the land of Israel would be restored to the Jews, who were exiled from it by the Romans, and also restored to the Palestinian Arabs who lived there before 1948. Not only is this impossible, but any attempt to secure the country for just one of these peoples would inflict suffering on millions whose only sin was being born in a contested land.

The Nobel Prize–winning novelist Kazuo Ishiguro offered a parable of the value of historical despair in his 2015 book *The Buried Giant*. The story follows an elderly couple making their way across Britain during the Dark

Ages, as they gradually realize that they are living amid the wreckage of a terrible war that no one seems to remember. Eventually they discover that King Arthur has put the land under a spell of oblivion, allowing Britons and Saxons to forget the massacres they inflicted on one another and live together in peace. When the spell is broken at the end of the book, the "buried giant" of historical hatred is awakened, and Ishiguro suggests that the consequences will be fearful: "Men will burn their neighbors' houses by night. Hang children from trees at dawn. The rivers will stink of corpses bloated from their days of voyaging."[6]

The magical forgetfulness in Ishiguro's story takes the form of mist breathed by a dragon. Those are hard to come by in the real world, but it's not necessary or even desirable for the past to be forgotten. On the contrary, when we lose track of what actually happened, we become vulnerable to purveyors of tendentious historical myths. Despairing of past injustices does not mean pretending they didn't happen, or that they were actually justice in disguise; it only means resolving that they should not be the cause of future injustices. In this sense, despair over the past is what makes it possible to hope for a better future, instead of perpetuating grievances and blood feuds.

In the case of the grievances raised by the ideology of settler colonialism, this ethic would mean recognizing that the European settlement of America should not be undone, but Native peoples should have the power to define and protect their way of life. The creation of the State of Israel should not be negated, but Palestinians should have the security and dignity of their own homeland. It would also mean accepting that while the creation of the United States and Israel was a curse to some people, it has been a blessing to many others. It is a sign of ignorance to turn any country into a symbol of evil, but in the case of these countries in particular, it is also a sign of ideological malice. And ideologues who "preach vengeance and murder from an ivory tower," in Rodinson's words, should be rebuked for their inhumanity, not praised for their idealism.

NOTES

Unless otherwise indicated, books were consulted via Kindle.

CHAPTER 1. THE THEORY OF A MASSACRE

1. "Approval and Mood of Country," Harvard CAPS–Harris Poll, December 13–14, 2023.
2. Ben Raab and Kaitlyn Pohly, "Petition to Oust Pro-Palestine Professor for 'Promoting Lies and Violence' Gains 25,000 Signatures in Just Over a Day," *Yale Daily News*, October 12, 2023.
3. Joseph Massad, "Just Another Battle or the Palestinian War of Liberation?" *Electronic Intifada*, October 8, 2023.
4. Jeffrey Sacks, "The Struggle Against Settler Colonial Affinities," *Mondoweiss*, October 18, 2023.
5. Paola Manduca et al., "An Open Letter for the People in Gaza," *Lancet* 384, no. 9941 (August 2, 2014).
6. "Israel's Religiously Divided Society," Pew Research Center, 2016.
7. Adam Dahl, *Empire of the People: Settler Colonialism and the Foundations of Modern Democratic Thought* (University Press of Kansas, 2018).
8. Amanda Morris, "What Is Settler Colonialism?", Learning for Justice, January 22, 2019.
9. Sacks, "The Struggle Against Settler Colonial Affinities."

10. Morris, "What Is Settler Colonialism?"

11. Sai Englert, *Settler Colonialism: An Introduction* (Pluto Press, 2017).

12. Leigh Patel, *No Study Without Struggle: Confronting Settler Colonialism in Higher Education* (Beacon Press, 2021).

13. Eve Tuck and K. Wayne Yang, "Decolonization Is Not a Metaphor," *Decolonization: Indigeneity, Education and Society* 1, no. 1 (2012).

14. Sofia Rubinson, "Cornell Professor 'Exhilarated' by Hamas's Attack Defends Remark," *Cornell Daily Sun*, October 16, 2023.

15. Pauline Wakeham, "The Slow Violence of Settler Colonialism: Genocide, Attrition, and the Long Emergency of Invasion," *Journal of Genocide Research* 24, no. 3 (2022).

CHAPTER 2. REDEFINING COLONIALISM

1. "The United Nations and Decolonization," United Nations, www.un.org/dppa/decolonization/en.

2. Kenneth Good, "Settler Colonialism: Economic Development and Class Formation," *Journal of Modern African Studies* 14, no. 4 (December 1976).

3. Patrick Wolfe, *Settler Colonialism and the Transformation of Anthropology: The Politics and Poetics of an Ethnographic Event* (Cassell, 1999).

4. Aimé Césaire, *Discourse on Colonialism*, trans. Joan Pinkham (Monthly Review Press, 2001).

5. Patrick Wolfe, "Settler Colonialism and the Elimination of the Native," *Journal of Genocide Research* 8, no. 4 (December 2006).

6. Lorenzo Veracini, "Introduction," in *The Routledge Handbook of the History of Settler Colonialism*, ed. Edward Cavanagh and Lorenzo Veracini (Routledge, 2017).

7. Wolfe, "Settler Colonialism and Elimination of the Native."

8. Raphael Lemkin, *Axis Rule in Occupied Europe* (Carnegie Endowment for International Peace, 1944).

9. Damien Short, *Redefining Genocide: Settler Colonialism, Social Death and Ecocide* (Zed Books, 2016).

10. Lorenzo Veracini, *Settler Colonialism: A Theoretical Overview* (Palgrave Macmillan, 2010).

11. Wolfe, *Settler Colonialism and the Transformation of Anthropology.*

12. Tuck and Yang, "Decolonization Is Not a Metaphor."

13. Mahmood Mamdani, *Neither Settler nor Native: The Making and Unmaking of Permanent Minorities* (Harvard University Press, 2020).

14. "Fast Facts," National Center for Education Statistics, NCES.ed.gov/fastfacts.

15. Ijeoma Nnodim Opara, "It's Time to Decolonize the Decolonization Movement," *PLOS Blogs | Speaking of Medicine and Health,* July 29, 2021.

16. Fiona Paisley, "White Settler Colonialisms and the Colonial Turn: An Australian Perspective," *Journal of Colonialism and Colonial History* 4, no. 3 (Winter 2003).

CHAPTER 3. A NEW AMERICAN COUNTERMYTH

1. Mahmood Mamdani, "Settler Colonialism: Then and Now," *Critical Inquiry* 41, no. 3 (Spring 2015).

2. "The Citizenship Act of 1924," Onondaga Nation, June 7, 2018.

3. Mamdani, *Neither Settler nor Native.*

4. Kyle Mays, "A Provocation of the Modes of Black Indigeneity: Culture, Language, Possibilities," *Ethnic Studies Review* 44, no. 2 (Summer 2021).

5. Laura Pulido, "Geographies of Race and Ethnicity III: Settler Colonialism and Nonnative People of Color," *Progress in Human Geography* 42, no. 2 (April 2018).

6. Horace Kallen, "Democracy vs. the Melting Pot," *Nation,* February 25, 1915.

7. Roxanne Dunbar-Ortiz, *Not "A Nation of Immigrants": Settler Colonialism, White Supremacy, and a History of Erasure and Exclusion* (Beacon Press, 2021).

8. Samuel Huntington, "Reconsidering Immigration: Is Mexico a Special Case?" Center for Immigration Studies, November 1, 2000.

9. Mamdani, *Neither Settler nor Native.*

10. Roxanne Dunbar-Ortiz, *An Indigenous Peoples' History of the United States* (Beacon Press, 2014).

11. Ned Blackhawk, *The Rediscovery of America: Native Peoples and the Unmaking of U.S. History* (Yale University Press, 2023).

12. Alfred A. Cave, *The Pequot War* (Amherst: University of Massachusetts Press, 1996), 105.

13. Richard J. Chacon and Rubén G. Mendoza, eds., *North American Indigenous Warfare and Ritual Violence* (University of Arizona Press, 2007).

14. Chacon and Mendoza, *North American Indigenous Warfare,* chapter 6.

15. Chacon and Mendoza, *North American Indigenous Warfare,* chapter 1.

16. Pekka Hämäläinen, *Indigenous Continent: The Epic Contest for North America* (Liveright, 2022).

17. Gary Snyder, *Turtle Island* (New Directions, 1974).

18. Hadeel Assali et al., "A Tradition of Defiance," *n+1*, October 26, 2023.

19. Amanda Robinson, "Turtle Island," *Canadian Encyclopedia*, November 6, 2018.

CHAPTER 4. SETTLER WAYS OF BEING

1. Robin D. G. Kelley, "The Rest of Us: Rethinking Settler and Native," *American Quarterly* 69, no. 2 (June 2017).

2. Englert, *Settler Colonialism*.

3. Tuck and Yang, "Decolonization Is Not a Metaphor."

4. Patel, *No Study Without Struggle*.

5. Dunbar-Ortiz, *Not "A Nation of Immigrants."*

6. Gerald Horne, *The Apocalypse of Settler Colonialism* (Monthly Review Press, 2017).

7. Alicia Cox, "Settler Colonialism," *Oxford Bibliographies*, 2017.

8. Wolfe, "Settler Colonialism and the Elimination of the Native."

9. Dunbar-Ortiz, *An Indigenous Peoples' History of the United States*.

10. "Why Columbus Day Courts Controversy," History.com, October 7, 2019.

11. Dunbar-Ortiz, *Not "A Nation of Immigrants,"* chapter 2.

12. Dunbar-Ortiz, *An Indigenous Peoples' History of the United States,* introduction.

13. Bram Wispelwey et al., "Towards a Bidirectional Decoloniality in Academic Global Health: Insights from Settler Colonialism and Racial Capitalism," *Lancet Global Health* 11, no. 9 (September 2023).

14. Anuradha Varanasi, "How Colonialism Spawned and Continues to Exacerbate the Climate Crisis," *State of the Planet: News from the Columbia Climate School*, September 21, 2022.

15. Jennifer Raff, *Origin: A Genetic History of the Americas* (Twelve, 2022).

16. Katherine G. Sammler and Casey R. Lynch, "Apparatuses of Observation and Occupation: Settler Colonialism and Space Science in Hawai'i," *Society and Space* 39, no. 5 (October 2021).

17. Robbie Shilliam, *Decolonizing Politics: An Introduction* (Polity Press, 2021).

18. Jacques Derrida, *Of Grammatology*, trans. Gayatri Chakravorty Spivak (Johns Hopkins University Press, 1997).

19. Rene Dietrich, "Made to Move, Made of This Place: 'Into America,' Mobility, and the Eco-Logics of Settler Colonialism," *Amerikastudien/ American Studies* 61, no. 4 (January 2016).

20. Kim TallBear, "Disrupting Settlement, Sex, and Nature," Indigenous Futures, 2016.

21. Ida Yoshinaga, "Disney's 'Moana,' the Colonial Screenplay, and Indigenous Labor Extraction in Hollywood Fantasy Films," *Narrative Culture* 6, no. 2 (Fall 2019).

22. Shawn Cuthand, "Introducing Yourself as a 'Settler' Creates Division," *CBC News Opinion*, August 30, 2021.

23. "Five Things You Can Do to Decolonize," American Friends Service Committee, May 10, 2019.

24. Lorenzo Veracini, "Decolonizing Settler Colonialism: Kill the Settler in Him and Save the Man," *American Indian Culture and Research Journal* 41, no. 1 (2017).

CHAPTER 5. THE PALESTINE PARADIGM

1. Nick Estes and Jaskiran Dhillon, eds., *Standing with Standing Rock: Voices from the #NoDAPL Movement* (University of Minnesota Press, 2019).

2. M. Muhannad Ayyash, "Israel Is a Settler Colony, Annexing Native Land Is What It Does," *Al Jazeera*, July 7, 2020.

3. Rachel Busbridge, "Israel-Palestine and the Settler Colonial 'Turn': From Interpretation to Decolonization," *Theory, Culture and Society* 35, no. 1 (January 2018).

4. Rashid Khalidi, *The Hundred Years' War on Palestine: A History of Settler Colonialism and Resistance, 1917–2017* (Metropolitan Books, 2018).

5. Joseph Massad, "Against Self-Determination," *Humanity Journal* 9, no. 2 (Summer 2018).

6. David Brion Davis and Steven Mintz, *The Boisterous Sea of Liberty: A Documentary History of America from Discovery Through the Civil War* (Oxford University Press, 1998).

7. "Jews Now a 47% Minority in Israel and the Territories, Demographer Says," *Times of Israel*, August 30, 2022.

8. "China: U.N. Experts Alarmed by Separation of 1 Million Tibetan Children from Families and Forced Assimilation at Residential Schools," Office of the United Nations High Commissioner for Human Rights, February 6, 2023.

9. "Chinese Persecution of the Uyghurs," U.S. Holocaust Memorial Museum.

10. Carole McGranahan, "Chinese Settler Colonialism: Empire and Life

in the Tibetan Borderlands," in *Frontier Tibet: Patterns of Change in the Sino-Tibetan Borderlands*, ed. Stéphane Gros (Amsterdam University Press, 2019).

11. Ruba Salih, Elena Zambelli, and Lynn Welchman, "'From Standing Rock to Palestine We Are United': Diaspora Politics, Decolonization and the Intersectionality of Struggles," *Ethnic and Racial Studies* 44 (2021).

12. Azeezah Kanji, "Canada and Israel: Partners in the 'Settler Colonial Contract,'" Yellowhead Institute, May 21, 2021.

13. Bram Wispelwey et al., "Because Its Power Remains Naturalized: Introducing the Settler Colonial Determinants of Health," *Frontiers in Public Health* 11 (2023).

14. "What Is Environmental Injustice and How Does It Affect Palestine?" Friends of the Earth, June 14, 2021.

15. Rosaura Sánchez and Beatrice Pita, "Rethinking Settler Colonialism," *American Quarterly* 66, no. 4 (December 2014).

16. Crispian Balmer, "Don't Preach to Us, Hamas Tells Secular West," Reuters, October 28, 2010.

17. Sarah Schulman, *Israel/Palestine and the Queer International* (Duke University Press, 2012).

18. Albert Memmi, *The Colonizer and the Colonized*, trans. Howard Greenfeld (Plunkett Lake Press, 2013).

19. Steven Salaita, *Inter/Nationalism: Decolonizing Native America and Palestine* (University of Minnesota Press, 2016).

20. Ahmad Amara and Yara Harawi, "Using Indigeneity in the Struggle for Palestinian Liberation," Al-Shabaka, August 8, 2019.

21. Steven Salaita, "Sheikh Jarrah: Zionism Distilled to Its Purest Expression," *Mondoweiss*, May 12, 2021.

22. Jamal Nabulsi, "Reclaiming Palestinian Indigenous Sovereignty," *Journal of Palestine Studies* 52, no. 2 (2023).

23. Richard Walther Darré, *A New Nobility of Blood and Soil*, trans. Augusto Salan and Julius Sylvester (Antelope Hill Publishing, 2021).

24. Salaita, *Inter/Nationalism.*

25. Wolfe, "Settler Colonialism and the Elimination of Native."

26. David Groulx, *From Turtle Island to Gaza* (Athabasca University Press, 2019).

27. David Nirenberg, *Anti-Judaism: The Western Tradition* (W. W. Norton, 2013).

28. Joseph Massad, "Nakba at 75: The Job of Israeli Settler Colonialism Is Never Done," *Middle East Eye*, May 16, 2023.

CHAPTER 6. WHY ISRAEL CAN'T BE DECOLONIZED

1. Maxime Rodinson, *Israel: A Colonial-Settler State?*, trans. David Thorstad (Monad Press, 1973).
2. Vladimir Jabotinsky, "The Iron Wall," Jabotinsky Institute in Israel, en.jabotinsky.org.
3. Palestinian Center for Policy and Survey Research, Public Opinion Poll no. 90, December 13, 2023, PCPSR.org/en/node/963.
4. Palestinian Center for Policy and Survey Research, Public Opinion Poll no. 80, June 15, 2021, PCPSR.org/en/node/843.
5. "Netanyahu Wants UNRWA Gradually Shut Down, Backs US Cuts," *Times of Israel*, January 7, 2018.
6. Tony Judt, "Israel: The Alternative," *New York Review of Books*, October 23, 2003.
7. Mamdani, *Neither Settler nor Native*.
8. Lorenzo Veracini, "The Other Shift: Colonialism, Israel, and the Occupation," *Journal of Palestine Studies* 42, no. 2 (Winter 2013).

CHAPTER 7. JUSTICE AND DESPAIR

1. John Collins, "Global Palestine: A Collision for Our Time," *Critique: Critical Middle Eastern Studies* 16, no. 1 (Spring 2007).
2. Walter Benjamin, *Illuminations: Essays and Reflections*, trans. Henry Zohn (Mariner Books, 1969).
3. *The New Science of Giambattista Vico*, trans. Thomas Goddard Bergin and Max Harold Fisch (Cornell University Press, 1968).
4. *The Aeneid*, book I, trans. John Dryden.
5. See *Bava Metzia* 21a–b, *Bava Kamma* 66a, *Bava Kamma* 114a–b.
6. Kazuo Ishiguro, *The Buried Giant* (Alfred A. Knopf, 2015).

SELECTED BIBLIOGRAPHY

Benjamin, Walter. *Illuminations: Essays and Reflections*, trans. Henry Zohn. Mariner Books, 2019.

Blackhawk, Ned. *The Rediscovery of America: Native Peoples and the Unmaking of U.S. History.* Yale University Press, 2023.

Cavanagh, Edward, and Lorenzo Veracini, eds. *The Routledge Handbook of the History of Settler Colonialism.* Routledge, 2017.

Chacon, Richard J., and Rubén G. Mendoza, eds. *North American Indigenous Warfare and Ritual Violence.* University of Arizona Press, 2007.

Dahl, Adam. *Empire of the People: Settler Colonialism and the Foundations of Modern Democratic Thought.* University Press of Kansas, 2018.

Dunbar-Ortiz, Roxanne. *An Indigenous Peoples' History of the United States.* Beacon Press, 2014.

———. *Not "A Nation of Immigrants": Settler Colonialism, White Supremacy, and a History of Erasure and Exclusion.* Beacon Press, 2021.

Englert, Sai. *Settler Colonialism: An Introduction.* Pluto Press, 2017.

Fanon, Frantz. *The Wretched of the Earth: 60th Anniversary Edition*, trans. Richard Philcox. Grove Press, 2021.

Hämäläinen, Pekka. *Indigenous Continent: The Epic Contest for North America.* Liveright, 2022.

Horne, Gerald. *The Apocalypse of Settler Colonialism.* Monthly Review Press, 2017.

Khalidi, Rashid. *The Hundred Years' War on Palestine: A History of Settler Colonialism and Resistance, 1917–2017*. Metropolitan Books, 2018.

Mamdani, Mahmood. *Neither Settler nor Native: The Making and Unmaking of Permanent Minorities*. Harvard University Press, 2020.

Memmi, Albert. *The Colonizer and the Colonized*, trans. Howard Greenfeld. Plunkett Lake Press, 2013.

Nirenberg, David. *Anti-Judaism: The Western Tradition*. W. W. Norton, 2013.

Patel, Leigh. *No Study Without Struggle: Confronting Settler Colonialism in Higher Education*. Beacon Press, 2021.

Raff, Jennifer. *Origin: A Genetic History of the Americas*. Twelve, 2022.

Rodinson, Maxime. *Israel: A Colonial-Settler State?*, trans. David Thorstad. Monad Press, 1973.

Salaita, Steven. *Inter/Nationalism: Decolonizing Native America and Palestine*. University of Minnesota Press, 2016.

Shilliam, Robbie. *Decolonizing Politics: An Introduction*. Polity Press, 2021.

Short, Damien. *Redefining Genocide: Settler Colonialism, Social Death and Ecocide*. Zed Books, 2016.

Veracini, Lorenzo. *Settler Colonialism: A Theoretical Overview*. Palgrave Macmillan, 2010.

Wolfe, Patrick. *Settler Colonialism and the Transformation of Anthropology: The Politics and Poetics of an Ethnographic Event*. Cassell, 1999.